Hermann Gross

Hermann Gross

Art and Soul

Robin Jackson

WIPF & STOCK · Eugene, Oregon

Wipf and Stock Publishers
199 W 8th Ave, Suite 3
Eugene, OR 97401

Hermann Gross
Art and Soul
By Jackson, Robin

Softcover ISBN-13: 979-8-3852-2229-2
Hardcover ISBN-13: 979-8-3852-2230-8
eBook ISBN-13: 979-8-3852-2231-5
Publication date 4/8/2024
Previously published by Floris Books, 2008

This edition is a scanned facsimile of the original edition published in 2008.

Contents

Foreword 7

Acknowledgments 8

1. Introduction 9

2. 1904–1928: Early years 11

3. 1928–1935: Paris 22

4. 1935–1940: Berlin 25

5. 1940–1945: Paris 27

6. 1946–1956: Paris and America 34

7. 1956–1963: Germany 47

8. 1963–1988: Scotland 49

9. Themes 58

 Religious works 59

 Masks and Masquerades 67

 Children and Camphill 77

 Camphill Hall 92

 Sketches 99

10. Conclusion 111

Bibliography 113

Index 116

Foreword

Although born in Germany like so many émigré artists of his day it was France that proved to be Hermann Gross' artistic homeland. Living there from 1926 he was immersed in the most cutting edge art of the time. The experience was to transform his work. Having returned to Berlin in 1935 it was perhaps ironic that Gross, having been drafted reluctantly into the German air force, should find himself posted to Paris, where once again he managed to make contact with the most significant artists of the day, including Pablo Picasso.

Many years later — when working in New York and subsequently in Scotland — this Parisian legacy remained powerful so that in his sculpture we can recognise the influence of Constantin Brancusi, whilst in some of his paintings we recall the delicacy of Marie Laurencin and in others the overpowering effect of Picasso or the dreamlike and visionary qualities of Marc Chagall.

Of all the artists working in Paris however it was the example of George Rouault which can be most clearly felt in the art of Hermann Gross. Rouault had trained as a painter and restorer of glass, which it has been suggested, was a likely source of the heavy black contouring and glowing colours which characterise his mature painting style. Like Gross he experimented in his early life with a variety of subjects — and was also clearly under the all-pervading influence of Picasso — but having dabbled with spiritualism and existentialism his art came truly into its own when he dedicated himself to Christian subjects. The same is true of Hermann Gross, for whom art and religion were inseparable.

It is therefore particularly apt that Robin Jackson assesses Gross' work within the context of the artist's deeply felt Christian beliefs which formed the basis of both his art and his life. These two strands were to prove fundamental, determining where Gross lived, how he lived and what he created. In 1963 the conjoined paths of art and religion led Hermann Gross to Aberdeen's Camphill community, a centre for people with special needs, where Gross became resident artist. Gross' work — so full of grace — echoed perfectly the anthroposophic philosophies of the Camphill movement. His contribution to the community was enormous and he has left an aesthetic legacy that even today, some 20 years after his death, pervades this special place. I am delighted that Robin Jackson has brought this long overdue monograph to fruition and that in so doing Hermann Gross' art can now be appreciated beyond the community that he held so dear.

Jennifer Melville
Keeper of Fine Art
Aberdeen Art Gallery and Museums

Acknowledgments

In writing this monograph I am grateful for the generous assistance given by Annelies Brüll, Anni D'Agostino, Stefan Geider, Christoph Hanni, Catherine Imhof-Cardinal, Mirjami Lyons and Marga Schnell of the Camphill Rudolf Steiner School, Aberdeen; Neil Curtis, Marischal Museum, University of Aberdeen; Melissa Buchanan, Andrew Martinez and Maureen O'Brien of the Museum of Art, Rhode Island School of Design; Kathy Kashmiry and Judy Throm of the Smithsonian Archives of American Art, Washington DC; Jonathon Jackson of the Special Collections Research Center, Syracuse University Library; Heather Brodhead, Santa Barbara Museum of Art, California; Bernd Ehlen, Wickersdorf, Germany; and Ron Morrell of Winchester, Virginia.

I am especially grateful to Christian Maclean, Catherine McKinney and Katy Lockwood-Holmes of Floris Books for translating this idea for a monograph into a reality. I owe a particular debt to Scott Dimond, Curator of the Southern Vermont Arts Center, Jennifer Melville, Keeper of Fine Art at Aberdeen Art Gallery and Margaret Crompton for so kindly finding the time to read and comment upon a draft version of the monograph. I am particularly grateful to my wife, Nancy, not only for the photographs of the Camphill Hall sculptures and stained glass windows but also for her very considerable assistance with all the illustrative material.

1. Introduction

Three years ago I knew absolutely nothing about Hermann Gross. In that regard I would have been no different from most other people. However, as a consultant to the Camphill Rudolf Steiner School in Aberdeen I became increasingly aware of the many paintings by Gross that hung in meeting rooms and family houses on the School's campus. Probably the key moment for me was when I was searching for an illustration for the cover of a book that I was in the process of editing which described the life and work of this Camphill community (Jackson, 2006). I wanted a picture that spoke directly to the viewer and which encapsulated the essence of Camphill philosophy and practice. With the help of The Hermann Gross Trust I was able to find exactly what I wanted. It was a painting which captured not only the central importance of the child in the Camphill community but also the quality of the care that was offered.

So impressed was I by this and other paintings that I became curious to learn more about the artist. During the course of my exploration I was invited to become a member of The Hermann Gross Trust. It was shortly after becoming a Trustee that I was asked if I would be interested in writing a book on Gross! It was only after agreeing to take on this commission that I began to realise the nature of the challenge. Whilst there had been two short private publications describing Gross' work and an obituary issue of *Camphill Correspondence* in which former colleagues recalled their memories of Gross, there was no other written material. Gross' name appears nowhere in European or American art history texts. I felt as if I had been given a map, which, on being opened up, had *terra incognita* written across most of it!

The impulse that drove me on was the conviction that the quality and range of Gross' work should be drawn to the attention of as wide an audience as possible. Subsequent confirmation that my judgement as to the quality of Gross' work was not misplaced stems from the fact that his work is now on display in the School of Education, University of Aberdeen and in 2007 an exhibition of some of his paintings was successfully staged by the Marischal Museum, University of

Aberdeen. Further, a silver head sculpted by Gross — an iconic work — has been accepted into the permanent collection of the Aberdeen Art Gallery.

At no point has writing this book been a burden. There are a number of reasons for this. Firstly, there is the extraordinary range of high technical skills displayed by Gross whether as sculptor, painter, silversmith or stained glass maker. Secondly, there are his contrasting life experiences from ballet dancer to Luftwaffe war artist, from being one of Picasso's pupils in Paris to artist-in-residence in a small lay community in Aberdeen. Thirdly, in following Gross' life we seem to be recording a spiritual odyssey. The fact that he should spend the last part of his life in an intentional community, which accords particular importance to the promotion of spiritual and aesthetic values, is not surprising. There is a sense in which Camphill was an inevitable destination!

This book is the first step in the exploration of the life and work of a very gifted artist whose talents have lain unrecognised for too long. My aim has been to share with readers the knowledge and insights I have gained in the hope that they, too, will come to appreciate the stature of Gross as man and artist.

2. 1904–1928: Early years

"The painting of a picture is no aesthetic matter. In so far as it is possible I would like it to be a communication from heart to picture and then from picture to heart, wherever such a contact is allowed."

Hermann Gross, January 1985. (Camphill Correspondence, 1989)

Hermann Gross was born on February 4th 1904 in Lahr in Baden-Württemberg. Lahr lies on the western edge of the Black Forest and is located less than 10 miles from the French border and is within sight of the Vosges Mountains. This close geographical proximity to France may well have had a profound effect on Gross' later life. When he was six, the family moved to Stuttgart, where he became a pupil at the *Realgymnasium*. When he left school in 1919, it was clear that Gross wanted to be an artist. From the age of 12 he had lessons in painting and drawing from an artist teacher. However, Gross' father, who had a publishing business, decided that in order to become an artist, his son would first need a solid grounding in a practical profession. He insisted that his wish be respected: so from 1919 until 1925 Gross attended the *Kunstgewerbeschule* (Art and Crafts School), where he learned to become a gold and silversmith. This training was to prove decisive and the skills acquired, particularly attention to detail, are evident in all his later work. Everything he did subsequently bears the hallmark of a thorough and accurate craftsman (Ehlen, 1989). (Plates 1–6)

In addition to his aptitude for art, Gross was also a first-class athlete. His special field was gymnastics and it is likely that he could have qualified for the German national team. However, this handsome youth wore his hair long and his clothing had a somewhat outlandish appearance — things which did not fit the image of what a German athlete should look like. He was, according to his own description, a hippy before his time. It may well have been his taste for the bohemian life that eventually attracted him to Paris (Ehlen, 2006).

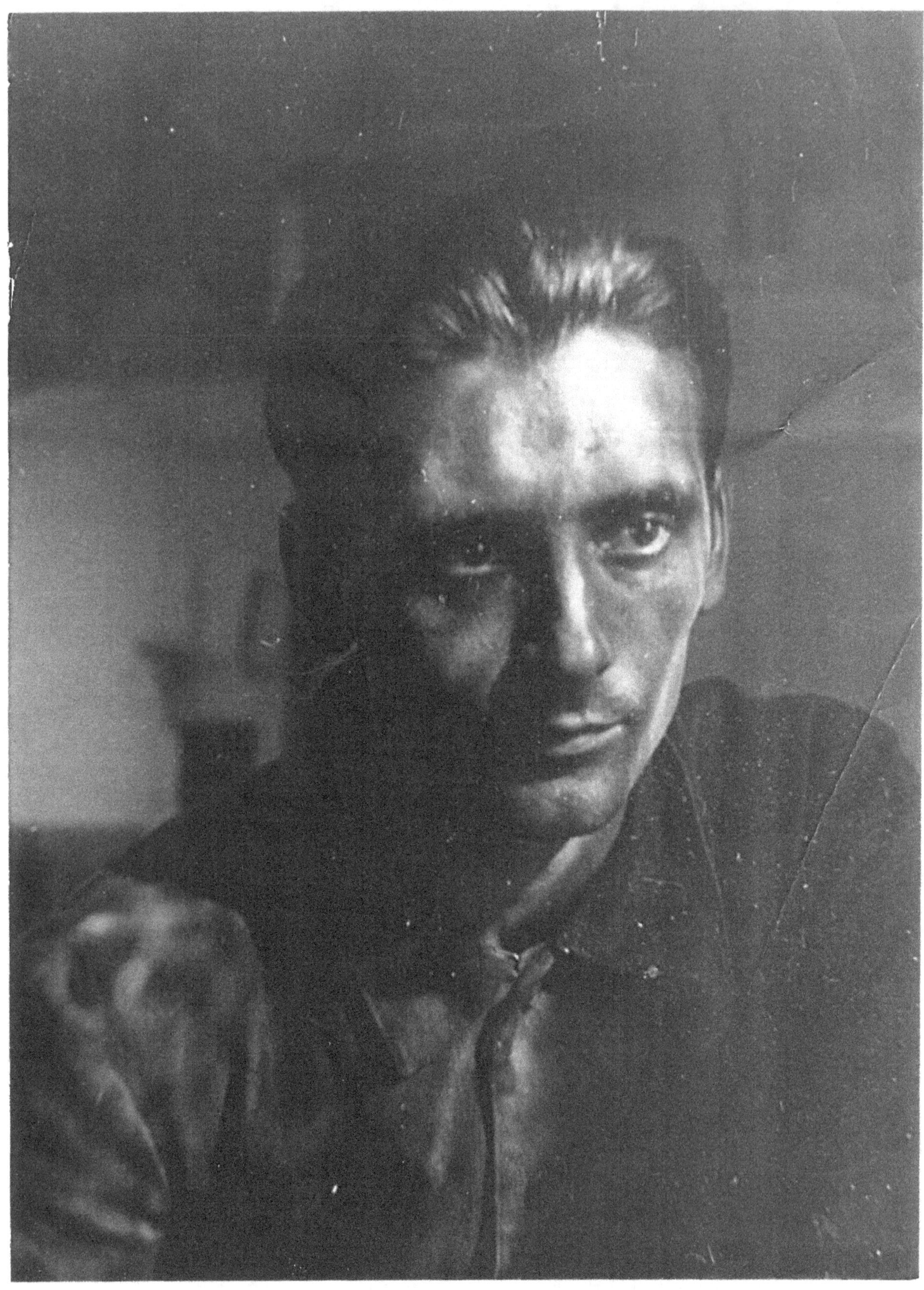

Plate 1

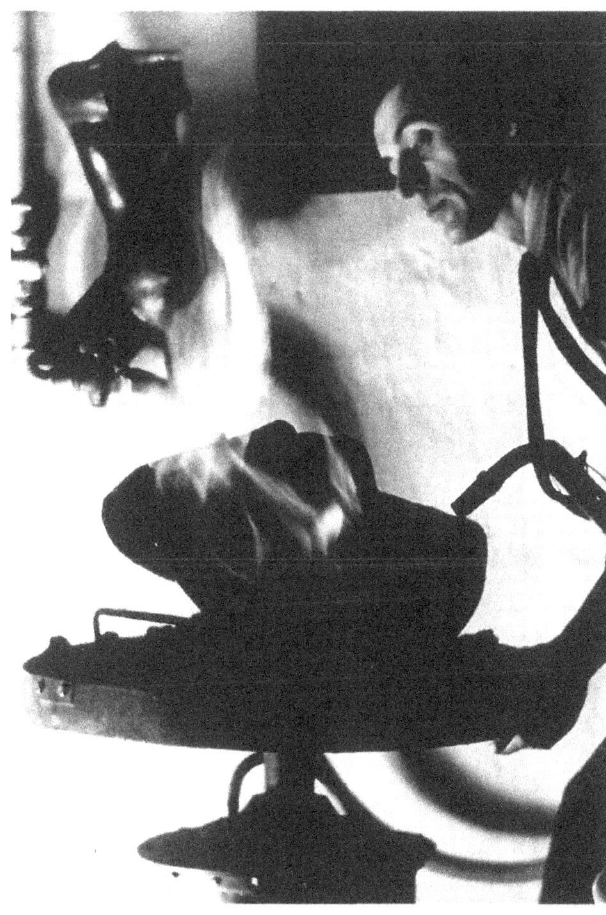

Left: Plate 2

Below: Plate 3

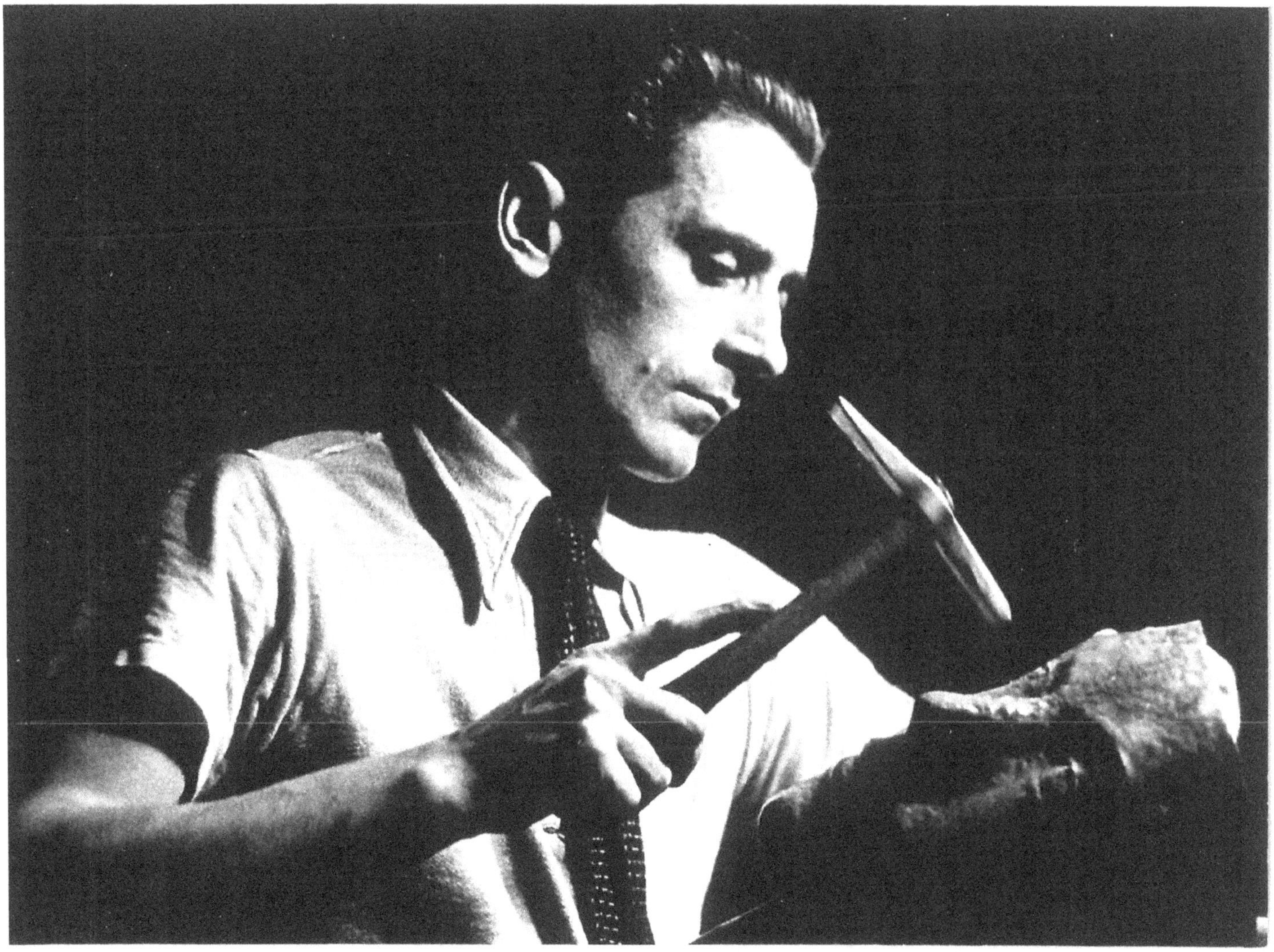

His friend, Hans Haustein, describes Gross as an outsider: "his remarkable page-boy hair cut soared above the high-necked collar of his black velvet suit, in which he moved about elegantly with small, quick steps: not surprisingly he knew how to dance the Charleston and the Blackbottom perfectly". According to Haustein, he would dance around the room which was on the top floor of his parents' apartment house with a cloth doll he had made himself, which had a somewhat sinister metal face mask. The room was full of bloodthirsty wall paintings which helped to create a solemn and hypnotic mood (Haustein, 1991).

Traumbühne Schertel

In 1925, at the age of 21, Hermann Gross appeared at the Munich Playhouse as a solo male dancer with the *Traumbühne Schertel* (Dream Theatre) — a modern dance group composed of young female dancers. The caption to a local newspaper review described the performance as '*Ein merkwürdiges Ballett*' — 'an odd ballet!' An intriguing feature of the review is that it includes a photograph of Gross wearing a mask and a cloak concealing his naked body. Masks were to feature as a leitmotif throughout Gross' life.

During the 1920s and 1930s modern dance and body culture in Germany converged on the pursuit of ecstasy, joyful release from the constraints of modern society and bourgeois convention. For women, modern dance was widely regarded as liberating. Many modern dancers were willing to dance nude in the name of art. However, there was considerable unease that such performances were likely to lead to the accentuation of sexual differences and eroticisation. It has been argued that the modern dance movement in Germany united artistic experimentation with attempts to create new modes of personal identity and communal life. It also challenged the traditional hierarchies of high and low culture (Toepfer, 1992; 1997).

Ernst Schertel (1884–1956) whose name was linked to this dance group was the mastermind behind the Parthenon publishing house in Leipzig and was a central figure behind the nudist movement (*Nacktkultur*) in Germany in the 1920s and 1930s. His magnum opus was *Der Flagellantismus als literalisches Motiv* (1929–1932) a pro-

Above: Plate 4

Below: Plate 5

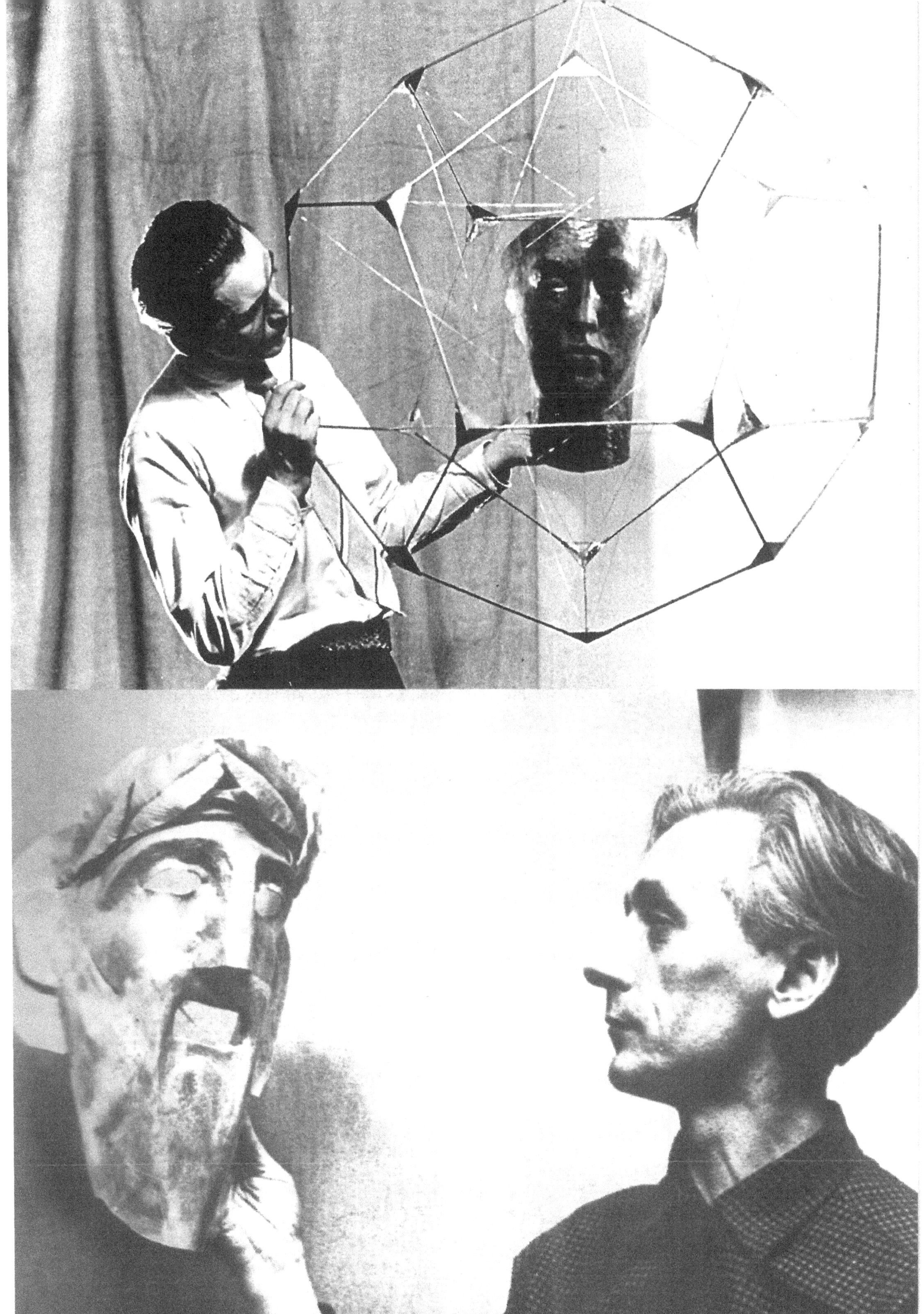

duction in four large volumes which he later supplemented with three more large volumes *Der erotischer Komplex* (1932). Schertel (1923) also wrote *Magic: History, Theory and Practice* an autographed copy of which he sent to Hitler where it formed part of Hitler's collection of 130 books on religious and spiritual subjects including Occidental occultism and Eastern mysticism. From the personal annotations and underlinings in this book, it appears that Hitler had read it very closely (Ryback, 2003).

The leading female dancer opposite Gross in the *Traumbühne* was the 15 year-old Toni van Eyck who went on to make a career in German films in the 1920s and 1930s. Her first film role was in *Spring Awakening* (1929) where she co-starred with Laszlo Loewenstein who, under his new name of Peter Lorre, played the archetypal villain in many well-known Hollywood movies (*Maltese Falcon*, 1941; *Casablanca*, 1942)! Another dancer with the *Traumbühne Schertel* at that time was Inge Frank who went on to become a teacher at the Bolshoi Ballet.

It is not known how Gross came to be involved with *Traumbühne Schertel* and why his excursion into this exotic arena appears to have been so short-lived. Maybe his father, who wanted his son to be well grounded in a practical profession, would not have been too enthusiastic about him embarking upon such an unconventional career. It is perhaps too simplistic to ascribe Gross' involvement as simply an expression of youthful exuberance or rebellion. Since he was from an early age of an artistic disposition, he would have been well aware of, and inevitably caught up in, the major cultural upheaval that was sweeping through Germany. This was not confined to the arts — painting, architecture, music, theatre, dance, film and literature — but extended more broadly to society as a whole — it was a social liberation movement. One of its most significant features was the drive to seek the sexual emancipation of women and what is beyond dispute is that the *Traumbühne* group was part of that emancipatory movement.

Gross' teachers

It is significant that the series of apprenticeships served by Gross in his early years were all spent with some of the most eminent practitioners in their respective fields in Europe. At the *Kunstgewerbeschule*, Gross attended silver and goldsmithing classes with Professor Paul Haustein, in due course becoming Haustein's

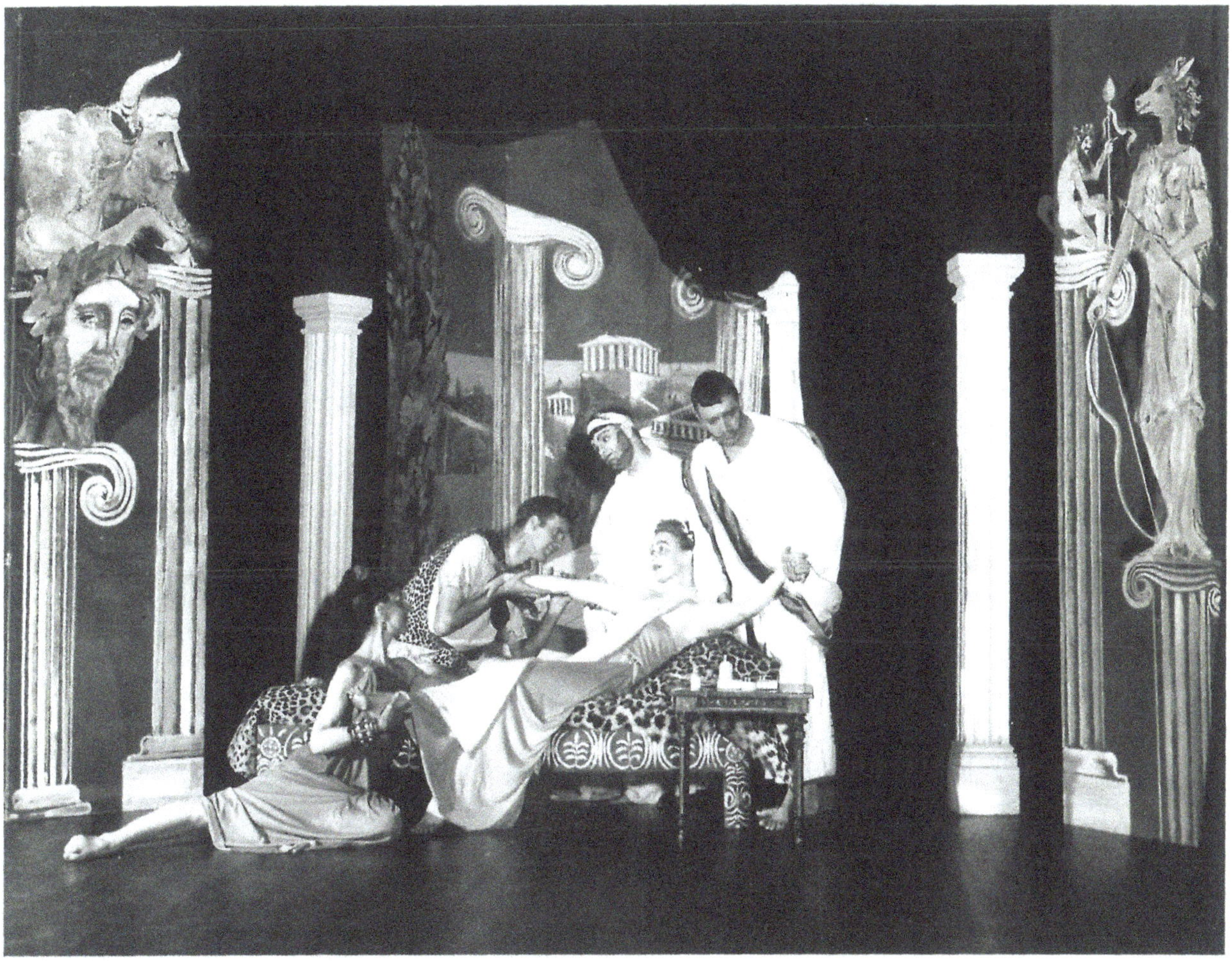

Plate 6

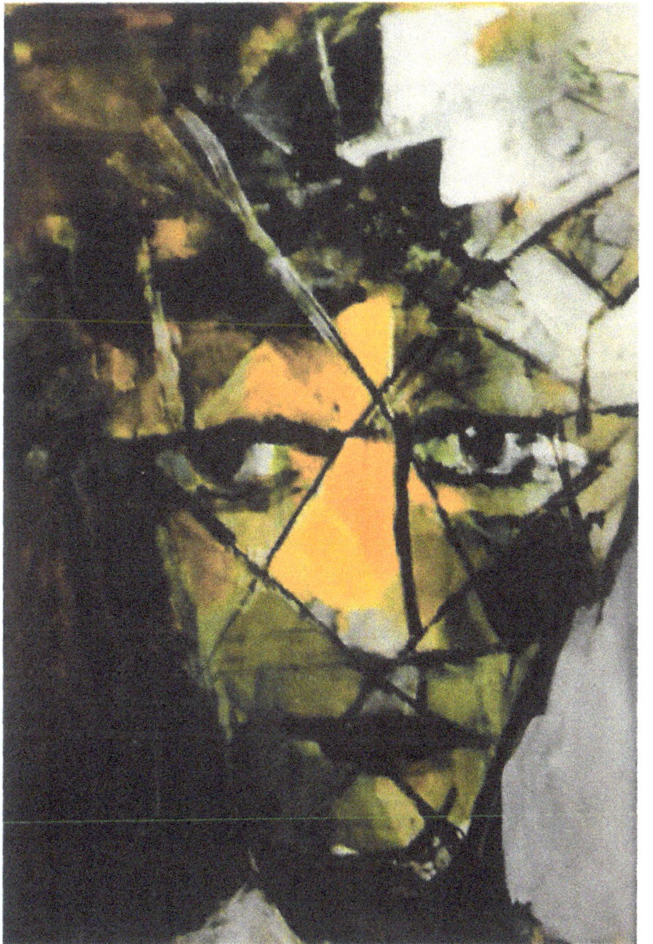

Plate 7

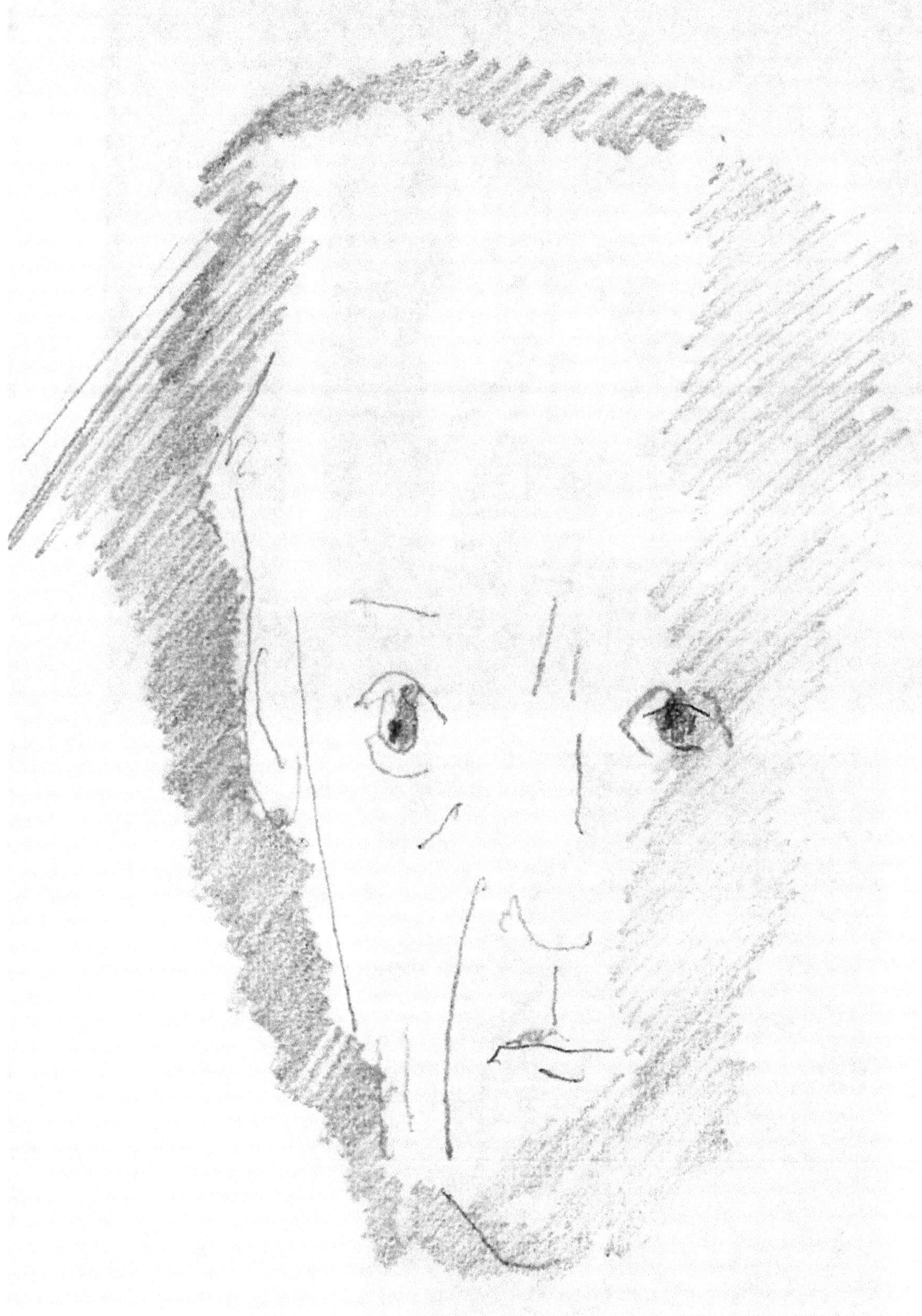

11.4.86

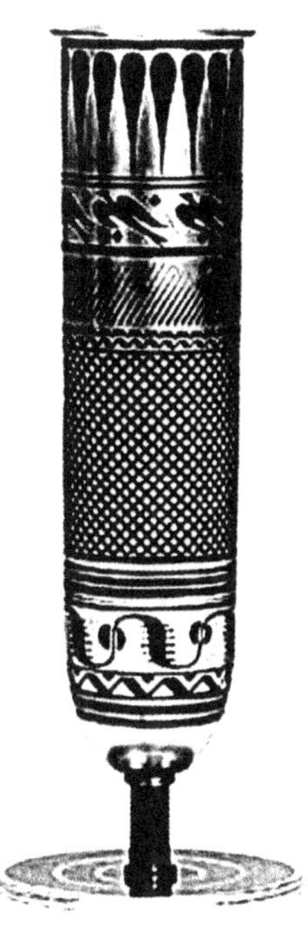

Plate 9

master pupil. In addition to his teaching commitments, Haustein, along with a number of other leading German designers, worked in a freelance capacity for WMF (*Württembergische Metallwarenfabrik*). WMF was one of the leading glass manufacturers in Europe in the 1920s and 1930s, responsible for pioneering the production of very high quality art glass (the *Ikora* and *Myra* designs), which gained a worldwide reputation. (Plate 9)

In 1925 Gross enrolled on a one-year course in engraving and metal-chasing run by Professor Waldemar Raemisch at the State Academy of Fine and Applied Arts in Berlin. Raemisch had begun his own career in Berlin as an apprentice in metalworking and sculpture. From 1919 to 1923, he taught at the High School of the Museum for Arts and Crafts and then became a professor at the State Academy of Fine and Applied Arts in Berlin. Working between the two world wars Raemisch designed, among other things: currency; public memorials; the German government's wedding gift to the Shah of Persia, and the bronze eagles at the entrance to the Olympic Stadium in Berlin. Forced from his professorship in 1937 because his wife was of Jewish descent, Raemisch emigrated to the USA. He was invited to the Rhode Island School of Design and officially took up post in September 1939. From 1946 to 1954 he was Head of the Sculpture Department (Buchanan, 2006). The two last bronze sculptures that Raemisch

Plate 8

completed are perhaps his best known. He was commissioned to provide sculptures representing the 'spirit of juveniles' which were to be located in front of the southwestern façade of the Youth Study Center on the Benjamin Franklin Parkway in Philadelphia. In each of the two groups, a seated figure is surrounded by idealized representations of children and attending adults. The central figures symbolize a universal Mother and a Doctor or Healer respectively — allegorical expressions of the care, comfort and guidance that adults can offer to children, (City of Philadelphia, 2008). (Plate 10)

In 1928 Gross moved to Paris where he worked with Robert Wlérick. Wlérick had begun his own artistic apprenticeship in 1899 at *L'École Municipale des Beaux-Arts* in Toulouse, where he had remained until 1904. In 1906 he left for Paris where he enrolled at *L'École des Beaux-Arts.* Wlérick exhibited for the first time at the *Salon de la Société Nationale des Beaux-Arts* in 1907. In Paris he joined the *Bande à Schnegg* — a group of sculptors seeking independence from the orthodox academic art taught in Art schools. Auguste Rodin, with whom several of them collaborated, supported them in this move. In 1929 Wlérick became professor at *L'Académie de la Grande Chaumière.* During the course of his life he received many prestigious commissions from the state, and his monumental works can be found in public places in Paris (Pomone; Athlete with Javelin). The work of Wlérick was greatly admired by Guillaume Apollinaire and Auguste Rodin, and it was Rodin who encouraged Wlérick to work in bronze. For Wlérick the purest subject of art was the human figure, as it represented for him a timeless beauty. (Plate 11)

Above: Plate 10

Below: Plate 11

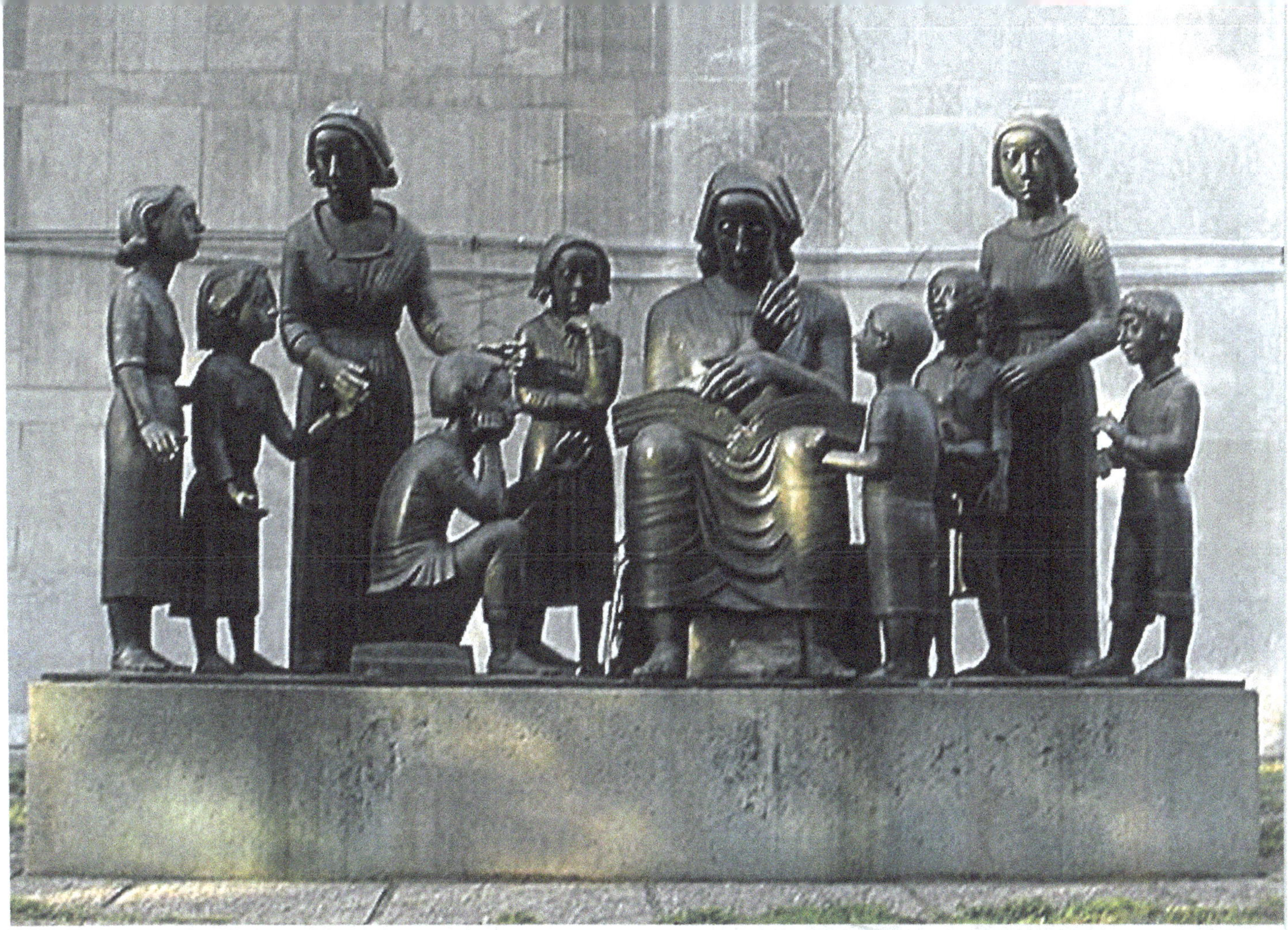

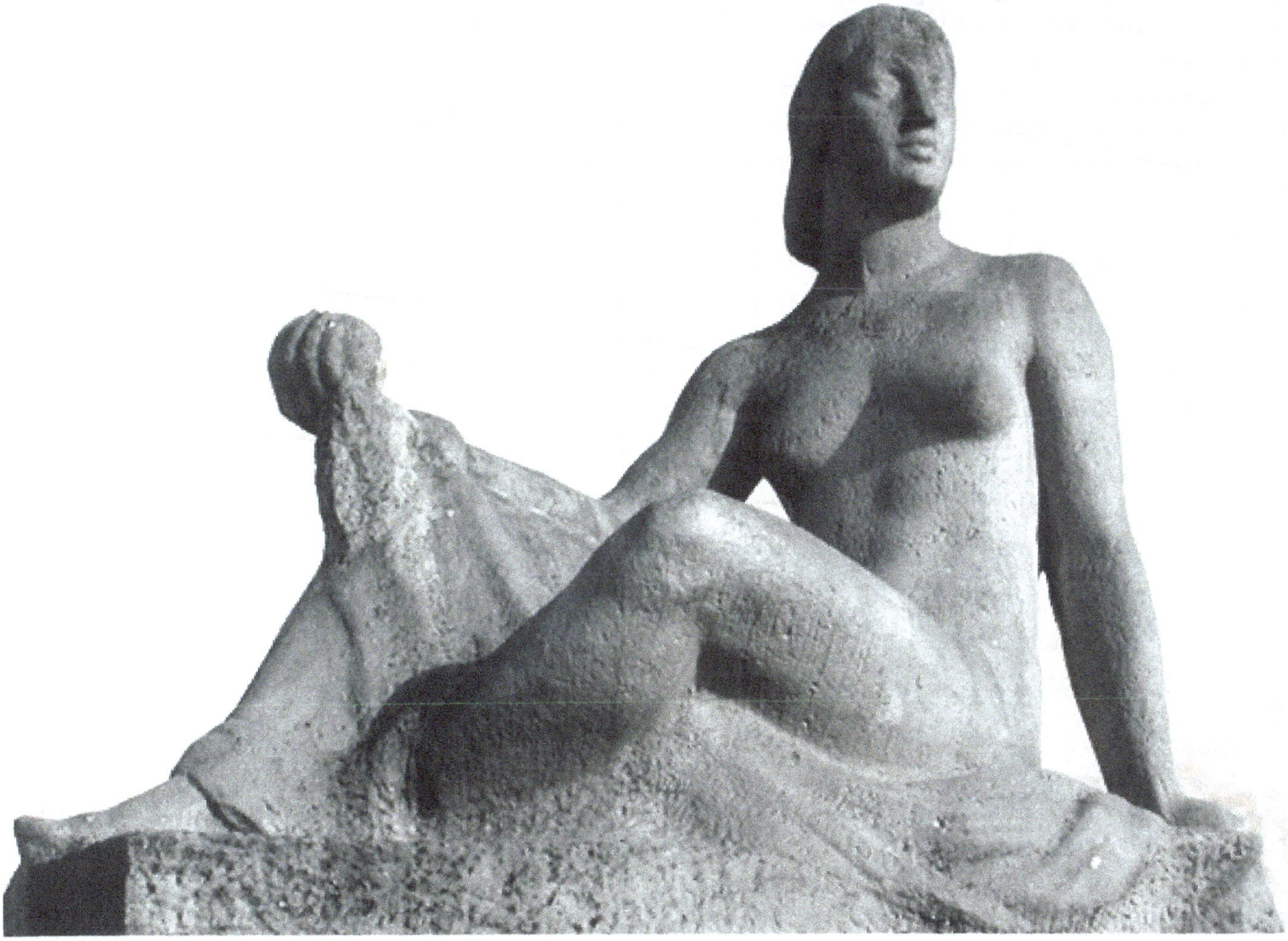

3. 1928–1935: Paris

When Gross moved to Paris in 1928 he was accompanied by his partner, Hildegard Friedrichs, author and fashion illustrator. They shared a shed-like building in a dreary courtyard at 48 Avenue des Gobelins bordering Montparnasse. Gross would often talk about how rundown and imperfect his studio was: the rain would come in and the lighting was bad. Nevertheless, he often compared his studio with the local restaurants where the paintwork and the wallpaper might be old and shabby and the plaster might be crumbling from the ceiling but the waiters were immaculately dressed and the food was excellent. That was very French and he loved it that way (Ehlen, 2006).

To those who knew him, Gross appeared perhaps more a Frenchman than a German. He spoke English with a distinct French accent, and altogether his whole manner and way of being had a strong French colouring. In France, Gross claimed, art always had its place. He is reported to have said: "In most countries, when people are faced with hard times, the arts suffer. When people struggle for their daily existence, art has to take a back seat. But not in France," (Ehlen, 2006).

According to Hans Haustein, his studio was full of fascinating items. The vice and the soldering equipment were surrounded by shelves filled with the steel heads of metalworking tools and hammers. Gross was a great admirer of French steel, especially from Thiers, which he rated highly for its purity and strength. A dodecahedron made of iron wire hung from the ceiling. Gross often used it as an instrument to check the scale and relative proportions of the small sculptures he was working on. The dilapidated walls were covered with pieces of paper full of sketches and figures, writing and photos. One particularly eye-catching object in the midst of this seeming confusion was a life-size portrait mask of the French cabaret artist — Suzy de Solidor. Gross was later to produce a gilded brass head of Suzy, (Haustein, 1991). (Plate 12)

Suzy de Solidor

Suzy de Solidor was a captivating character who was at the heart of Parisian nightlife. She was born in Deauville in 1900. She changed her name from Suzy Louise Rocher to Suzy de Solidor when she moved to Paris in the late 1920s. She was one of the first symbols of sexual emancipation in France during the 1930s. Early in 1930, she became popular as a singer, opening a chic nightclub called *Boîte de Nuit* which was one of the trendiest night spots in Paris. Suzy Solidor did not hide her sexuality and sang songs that overtly revealed that she was gay. One of the singer's most famous publicity achievements was to become heralded as 'the most painted woman in the world'. She posed for some of the best-known artists of the day including Jean Cocteau, Pablo Picasso and Georges Braque. Her stipulation for sitting was that she would be given the paintings to hang in her club. There are, in total, around 150 paintings of Solidor. In Cagnes-sur-Mer, in the south of France, there is a museum dedicated to her with a collection of 42 portraits, all painted by different artists. She died in 1983.

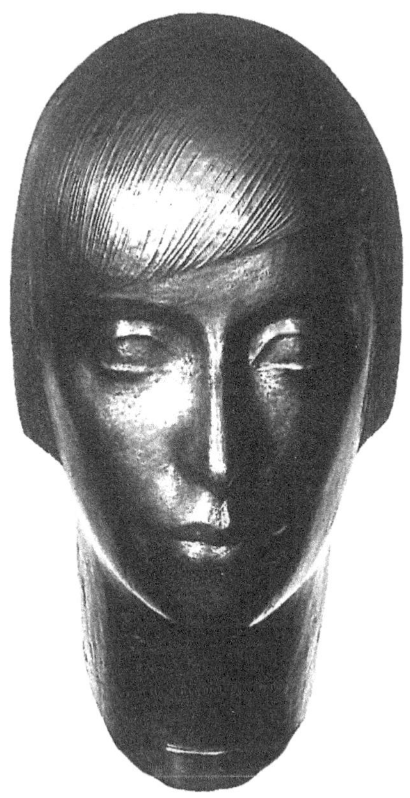

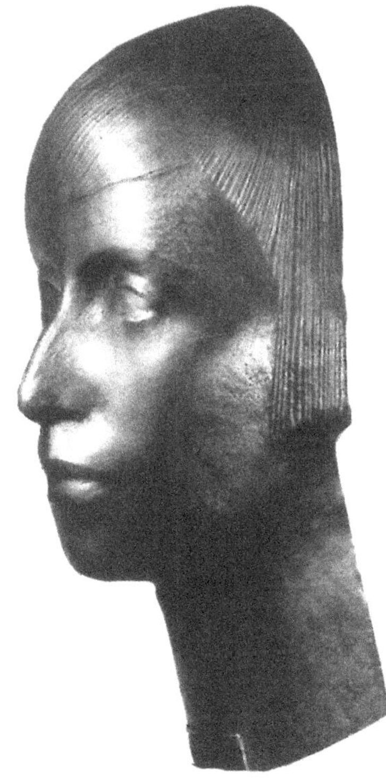

Plate 12

It is not known whether Suzy de Solidor sat for Gross or whether he based his work on occasional sightings of her at cabaret performance or on the many paintings of her that would have been accessible in Paris at that time. If Gross owes an artistic debt to anyone at this stage of his career it would appear to be to Constantin Brancusi — one of the founding figures of modern sculpture, who was living in Paris. Brancusi's groundbreaking carvings introduced abstraction and primitivism into sculpture for the first time. The striking feature of Gross' sculpture is the way in which he has captured the androgynous character of Suzy through a simplification and progressive refining of her facial features; at the same time Gross appears to have captured the essence of her personality. An argument can also be advanced that this work reveals a strong art deco influence. In 1925 the Éxposition des Arts Decoratifs et Industriels was held in Paris. Whilst it is not known if Gross visited the Éxposition, it would have been impossible for him to have been unaware of the great impact that the art deco style had on painting, sculpture and architecture.

Gross had a circle of friends in Paris — mostly young people at the beginning of their artistic careers. Among them was Jean-Louis Barrault, who became one of France's most distinguished French actors and directors — perhaps best remembered for his portrayal of Hamlet and as the mime in Marcel Carné's film *Les enfants du paradis* (1944).

It is known that Gross, who lived near to Montparnasse, knew Picasso (Schnell, 2006) and Matisse (Ehlen, 2006). And it seems highly probable, given the number of years he spent in this small Paris district, that he was also acquainted with Chagall and Braque. In 1929 Gross exhibited at the *Salon d'Automne* in Paris a metal sculpture entitled *Portrait de jeune fille repoussé sur cuivre* (Salon d'Automne, 2006). One Parisian art critic observed that his work 'has a soul of the most perfect nobility.' The first *Salon d'Automne* had been organised by Rouault, Derain and Matisse in 1903 as a reaction to the conservative policies of the official Paris *Salon*. The exhibition almost immediately became the showpiece of developments and innovations in 20th century painting and sculpture. After World War I the *Salon d'Automne* was dominated by the works of Montparnasse painters such as Chagall, Modigliani and Braque.

4. 1935–1940: Berlin

In 1935 Gross left Paris and returned to Berlin, as his father was seriously ill. His return to Germany, which was now under the Nazi regime, was also probably prompted by other changes in his personal life; he and Hildegard Friedrichs had separated, he was suffering from a sense of alienation and missing his German friends (Haustein, 1991). Gross and Hans Haustein rented an attic studio at 32 Landsbergerstrasse in North East Berlin, in a working-class neighbourhood not far from the Alexanderplatz. Reached by a gloomy staircase leading past a number of small businesses, the studio was divided into two parts by a large sliding door; daylight came through skylights and side windows. The social background of the people living in the courtyard below made them the sworn enemies of the Nazis. Among Gross' neighbours was a signwriter and a coal merchant, both of whom had helped the previous tenant of the studio, Theodor Plivier, to evade the Gestapo. Plivier, a Marxist, was to write the epic novel *Stalingrad* (1948) which has been regarded as one of the classics of anti-war literature ranking alongside *All Quiet on the Western Front* (Remarque, 2005) and *Born on The Fourth of July* (Kovic, 1976). It describes the crushing defeat of the German Sixth Army, and became an international best seller. The only notice that Plivier's writing attracted in Germany itself came from the Nazi Party, which banned his books in 1933 and revoked his citizenship in 1934. In 1933, Plivier fled to Moscow, only returning to the West in 1947.

Gross' studio became a meeting place for many people with similar interests. The women journalists Trude Sand and Martha Hillers belonged to this circle of friends. Martha Hillers later married Karl Dietschy, a jeweller from Basel, who became a very good friend of Gross, as well as a patron who commissioned his metal sculptures (Haustein, 1991). Martha has been revealed as the anonymous author of *A Woman in Berlin: Eight Weeks in the Conquered City — A Diary* which described the horrors that war brought to the lives of the women in Soviet-occupied Berlin (Hillers, 2006). It has recently been reprinted and is a bestseller in the USA and UK. Other members of the circle included the publisher Günther

Wasmuth who was responsible in 1929 for the production of a four-volume encyclopaedia on architecture — *Lexikon der Baukunst* (Wasmuth, G., 1929) — and his brother Ewald, a philosopher, and translator of the works of Pascal (Wasmuth, E., 1946).

5. 1940–1945: Paris

According to an interview given to William Dunbar of the *Scottish Sunday Express* in October 1963, Gross was conscripted into the Luftwaffe and trained as an air gunner (Dunbar, 1963). "Fortunately", according to Gross, "I was medically discharged before I saw any action. You see, I could not have killed anyway. I felt too strongly that man's mission on earth was to create, not to destroy". It is clear from existing documentary records that Gross was not discharged from the Luftwaffe but served subsequently as a war artist in one of Goering's Propaganda Companies based in Paris. The question arises as to the reasons for the medical discharge. On his own admission it is clear that Gross would not have made a very effective air gunner thus putting the lives of the rest of the aircrew at risk. His discharge was most probably on the grounds of psychological unfitness for the task. His selection for a Luftwaffe propaganda unit almost certainly resulted from his specialist knowledge and expertise.

Given his location in Paris in 1940 and his membership of a propaganda unit, it would have been impossible for Gross not to have known of the existence of the *Einsatzstab Reichsleiter Rosenberg* (ERR) unit and what it was doing. Hermann Goering established this unit in 1940 and it was the official Nazi office charged with confiscating important, mainly Jewish, art collections in the western Nazi-occupied territories. ERR was housed in the *Jeu de Paume Museum* in Paris and operated there from 1940 to 1944. It is believed to have looted more than 21,000 individual objects from over 200 Jewish-owned collections. By 1945 Goering possessed over 2000 individual pieces, including more than 1300 paintings. The fact that Gross was a witness of, and indirectly complicit in, the wholesale plundering of the artistic heritage of the city he loved by his own countrymen must have had a devastating psychological effect upon him. Further, the fact that his own work and that of the artists he most admired — Matisse, Picasso, Braque — were regarded as degenerate by the authorities would have been hard to bear.

But that official distaste for the work of modern French and German artists was not new. Soon after their rise to power in 1933, the Nazis purged so-called 'degenerate art' from German public institutions and started to close art schools. The Nazis were anxious to rid Germany of all the art created during the Weimar Republic, the period from 1924 to 1930, when Germany was a leading European cultural centre, especially in the fields of art, cinema and literature.

Gross' work in the propaganda unit involved him in a wide variety of activities. One of the more bizarre tasks he was called upon to undertake was to 'doctor' photographs of air battles. Photographs would be rearranged so as to show successfully attacking Hurricanes or Spitfires being caught in a hail of imaginary bullets from diving and triumphant Messerschmitts or Heinkels. These fake pictures had then to be approved by the propaganda section before being sent to the newspapers for printing. The faking of the photographs had to be done very speedily so that no-one would suspect the deception. The German people would then be provided with 'evidence' not only of the supremacy of the Luftwaffe but also the magnificent achievements of Reichsmarschall Goering, head of the Luftwaffe. The truth was that, during the course of what later was to be called the Battle of Britain, the Luftwaffe was sustaining heavy losses, knowledge of which would certainly have dented national morale (Ehlen, 2006).

Members of the Luftwaffe propaganda units were accorded certain privileges that were denied other servicemen: the most obvious being that they were equipped with pencils as opposed to rifles and expected to engage in creative as opposed to destructive work. Such privileges may have represented payment for their silence because they would be among the few who would have known what was really happening.

Ten photographs of sketches drawn by Gross whilst serving in the propaganda unit were found recently among his personal papers. It remains a mystery that Gross was able to photograph this sensitive material and then keep copies of it. There can be no doubt as to their authenticity as they still have the official Luftwaffe tickets attached. From these tickets, it appears that Gross was an *Obergefreiter* (Royal Air Force equivalent of Leading Aircraftman) and a member of *Luftwaffe Propaganda-Kompanie 3* and engaged as a *Pressezeichner* (press draughtsman). Propaganda companies usually consisted of reporters, radio commentators, photographers, cameramen and artists, whose duty it was to secure reports of troops in action, for publication by press and radio and to take film for inclusion in newsreels.

All the drawings concerned the defences being constructed along the French north coast — Hitler's Atlantic Wall (*Kanalküste*). From the topography it appears we are looking at the chalk cliffs somewhere along the Normandy coast. Hitler's Wall was intended to reduce German military weakness in the West and thereby deter or impede an Allied invasion. The work on the Wall was undertaken from late 1942 to the summer of 1945. The *Todt Organization*, a semi-independent agency under the Ministry of Armaments, was responsible for the Wall's construction. By 1943, 250,000 workers poured up to 800,000 tons of concrete monthly into sophisticated fortifications, some of immense proportions. In the period 1942–1944, the Germans used over 17 million cubic metres of concrete and 1.2 million metric tons of steel for the Atlantic Wall. Whilst Adolph Hitler boasted that he was the greatest fortress builder of all time, he never once visited the Channel fortifications.

Are these carefully drawn sketches simple and straightforward representations of what lay before Gross, or instead was he trying to communicate a hidden message, which if it had been detected would almost certainly have resulted in harsh punishment — possibly death? If it was the latter what was it that drove Gross to act in this way? It is doubtful if there was any one factor. He would have been angered at the dismissal by the Nazis of most of modern art as 'degenerate' — particularly the work of those Jewish artists like Chagall, Modigliani and Soutine who he particularly admired. The wholesale pillaging of the art treasures of Paris by the Nazis that he witnessed would have depressed him, as Paris had been his beloved spiritual home. There is perhaps a certain irony in the fact that as a failed air gunner, he was nevertheless able to fire at key targets in such a devastatingly accurate manner!

Presumably the intention in the first sketch (Plate 13) is to take the bunker as the principal focal point, yet it is what lies beside the bunker that catches our attention. Is it accidental that in this sketch the discarded planks that lie alongside the bunker have fallen in the shape of a cross? At the top of the central plank there is a circle of barbed wire. Is it too far fetched to imagine this as the crown of thorns on Christ's brow? After the war Gross was obsessed with producing an endless series of dark brooding pictures of the crucifixion and resurrection. In

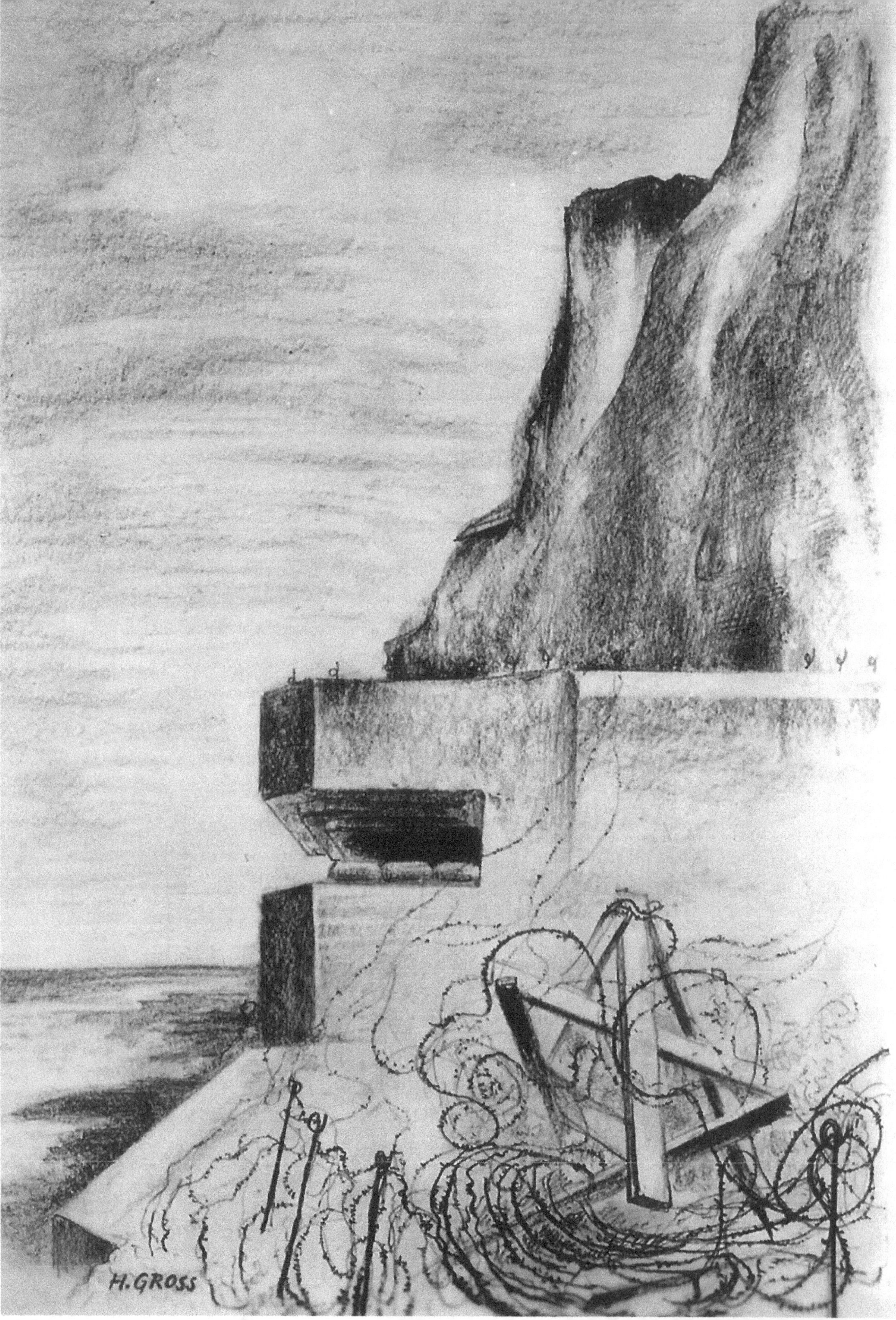
H.GROSS

studying the planks entangled in the barbed wire, is it also possible to detect a distorted Star of David swathed in barbed wire? Might this be an allusion to the internment of Jews and others in concentration camps?

What else might this sketch be saying? We are presented with a reinforced and sharply angular concrete building, the simplicity, functionality and brutality of which mirror features of Bauhaus architecture. It is ironic that Bauhaus architecture was discredited by the Nazi regime not least because of its association with the Weimar Republic. A feature of the bunker itself is that the observation platform is empty. We have a skull-like construction that is eyeless and lacking vision.

A curious aspect of this sketch is the haphazard way in which the barbed wire lies alongside the bunker. It seems improbable that any self-respecting German soldier would have tolerated such an inadequate and untidy defensive structure. One is tempted to conclude that Gross used artistic licence here to make a point. Whilst the bunker sketched by Gross gives all the appearance of something solid and permanent, the chalk cliffs behind it, which Gross highlights, remind us that nothing is enduring in the face of the sea. And so it has proved, for most of the 15,000 bunkers and other defensive fortifications built along the Channel coast are in the process of disintegration, having been affected by erosion and rock falls. Was Gross implying that tyrannies, like bunkers, do not last forever?

The meticulously clean, bloodless and aseptic tiled underground operating theatre seen in Plate 14 is striking for a number of reasons. All the soldiers, including the person who is being operated upon, are accoutred in incongruously shiny jackboots a symbol later to be applied to cruel and authoritarian behaviour or rule. There is a high degree of irony here too in that even jackbooted soldiers are revealed as vulnerable and require dedicated care and attention in order to survive. The operation is conducted adjacent to a cupboard on which there is what one must assume to be a Red Cross — the symbol that is placed on humanitarian and medical vehicles and buildings to protect them from military attack! Whilst there is always a danger of reading too much into a drawing, it is noticeable that the stability of the trolley upon which this delicate operation is being performed is dependent on the cross bracing joining the legs. Without such cross bracing the table would collapse. Put another way, without the cross (i.e., Christianity), civilization will collapse.

Plate 13

In Plate 15 it is tempting to see the three gigantic concrete mixers that are located at the top of a hill as a grotesque representation of Calvary — the site of Christ's crucifixion. The paradox here is that the three mixers are only kept 'alive' through the nonstop efforts of slave labour. We are witnessing a modern day 'crucifixion' in which many of those working on these sea defences died. The inference that this sketch may be an allusion to Calvary is strengthened by reference to the succession of sketches that Gross drew of crucifixion scenes after the war.

Was Gross seeking to communicate hidden messages in these sketches? Art in Northern Europe has been rich in hidden symbolism. For example, in the 15th century Jan van Eyck and Rogier van der Weyden, two masters of Northern Renaissance art, used symbols to communicate messages which would have been viewed as heretical and subversive if spoken or written at that time (Harbison, 1995). Through their art they were able to allude to the kind of shortcomings in the Catholic Church that Martin Luther later condemned (e.g., van Eyck's *Virgin and Child with Chancellor Rolin*: 1433 Musée du Louvre, Paris and van der Weyden's *The Seven Sacraments*: 1445–50 Koninklijk Museum voor Schone Kunsten, Antwerp). This was risky because their livelihood depended to a significant degree on church patronage. They were taking a gamble just as Gross was doing; however the stakes for Gross were much higher, as he was commenting critically not only about the brutal character of the Nazi regime but also its antipathy to art and religion.

Towards the end of the war, Gross was posted to Poland and Russia, where he served as a guard for the command headquarters. There he had to endure bitterly cold winters with inadequate clothing and equipment. Whether Gross' subsequent transfer to the Eastern Front stemmed from official concerns raised by his work as a war artist will never be known. It is more likely that the transfer was part of a major deployment of military personnel from the Western to the Eastern Front which was crumbling in the face of the remorseless Russian advance. It is not known how he managed to return to Germany after the collapse of the Eastern Front and the subsequent rout of the German army. However we do know that his studio in Landsbergerstrasse, Berlin, was completely destroyed in an air raid in 1945.

Above: Plate 14

Below: Plate 15

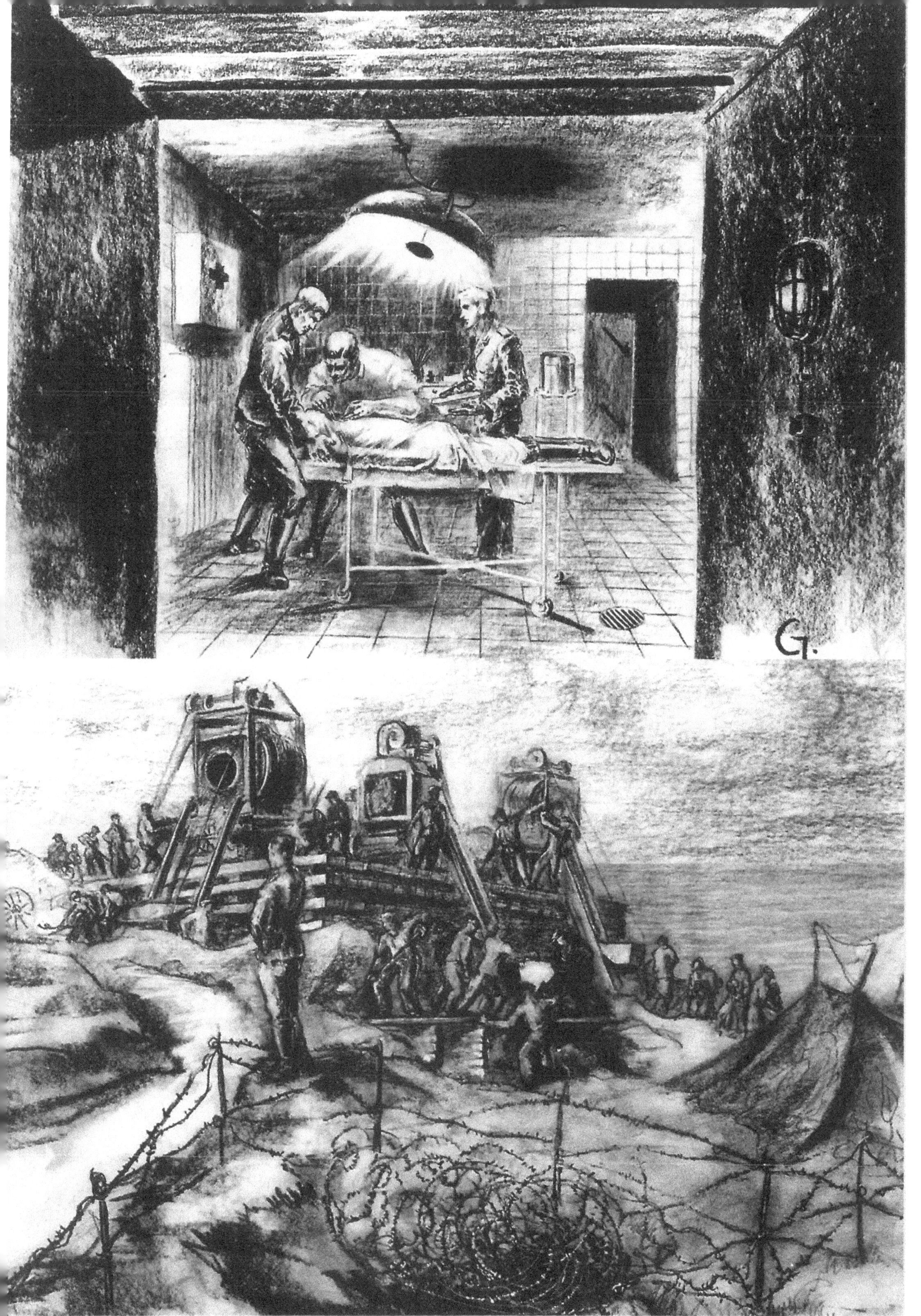
G.

6. 1946–1956: Paris and America

Gross returned from the war in a very poor psychological condition and for a time lived a quiet and humdrum middle-class existence that was quite at odds with his true character. According to a brief CV produced by Gross, he had an exhibition of his work at the Stadthaus in Freudenstadt in Baden-Württemberg in 1946. Freudenstadt is significant for two reasons. Firstly, Hildegard Rath who was later to become his wife was born in Freudenstadt on 22 March 1909. Secondly, from 1942 to 1947 Rath ran the Art House in Freudenstadt. So it is possible that he met his wife-to-be in Freudenstadt. In 1946 Gross returned to Paris where he resumed work as a painter and sculptor. It seems likely that Rath accompanied him as she produced a series of painting of Parisian scenes at that time. In 1948 they married and in that same year left France for America. It is known that Rath had visited America in 1937 and stayed a year with her brothers, Walter and Dolf, who lived in Vermont.

Their decision to emigrate was probably prompted by several considerations. It is doubtful if the presence of two Germans in Paris in the immediate aftermath of a war that had devastated the French capital would have been entirely welcomed. Paris of 1946 would have been a totally different place, culturally, socially and politically, to the Paris of 1926. Rath had probably received encouragement from her brothers to emigrate to the USA and having some knowledge of the superior quality of life that was on offer on the other side of the Atlantic and having experienced post-war austerity in Western Europe, the pull proved too great. Given Gross' traumatic experiences during the war, it may also have been thought that a totally new environment would speed his rehabilitation. Finally, the USA offered more opportunities to further their respective careers as artists.

Hildegard Rath

Rath played an important role in Gross' life whilst he was in the USA, not least as a determined advocate of his work. Her father was a president of a bank, her mother a sculptor, writer and illustrator of children's books. At the age of 15, she painted her first portrait in oils as a birthday present for her father and thereafter every opportunity for study was given to her. This included private instruction by Impressionist Adolph Senglaub at the Atelier House in Stuttgart and at the Akademie der Bildenen Kunste in Berlin. She studied with Otto Manigk and then Lotte Laserstein. Otto Manigk was one of a number of German artists who specialised in the depiction of the ever-changing sea and skyscape of the Baltic Sea Coast in particular the island of Usedom — an island that exercises a strong physical and metaphysical attraction to Germans. Indeed since the end of the 19th century the Baltic coastline has been a favourite destination for many artists including Edvard Munch. A book of Manigk's paintings has recently been published by the State Museum in Schwerin (von Berswordt-Wallrabe, 2001).

Lotte Laserstein was one of the foremost German female artists working between the two World Wars. She was one of the first women to be accepted at the Berliner Kunstacademie in 1919, where she graduated with honours in 1927. The character of her paintings was cosmopolitan, self-confident and modern and fitted the melancholic feeling of *Sachlichkeit* (Realism/Objectivity) current in Germany at that time. Men rarely featured in her universe, as she tended to paint self confident, urban and athletic women who played sport, attached importance to their appearance and went unaccompanied to restaurants. These were young women who were truly emancipated. It is generally accepted that Laserstein's masterpiece was the atmospheric and enigmatic 1930 painting *Abend über Potsdam*, a frieze of friends enjoying a meal on their terrace, with Potsdam's skyline in the far distance.

Rath travelled extensively throughout Europe and the USA. Her preferred media were oil, pastel, watercolour and charcoal and she became a painter of landscapes, portraits, still lifes, city scenes, dreams and visions. (Plates 16 and 17) In Germany she had numerous commissions for oil paintings in the 1930s and 1940s. She was very active in exhibitions during most of her life in the USA and Europe and she received a number of international awards for her work including the prestigious Prix de Paris in 1963 and a gold medal from the *Accademia Italia delle Arti e del Lavoro* in 1980. In September 1963 she wrote an article for the leading American art magazine — *American Artist.* (Rath, 1963). She was listed

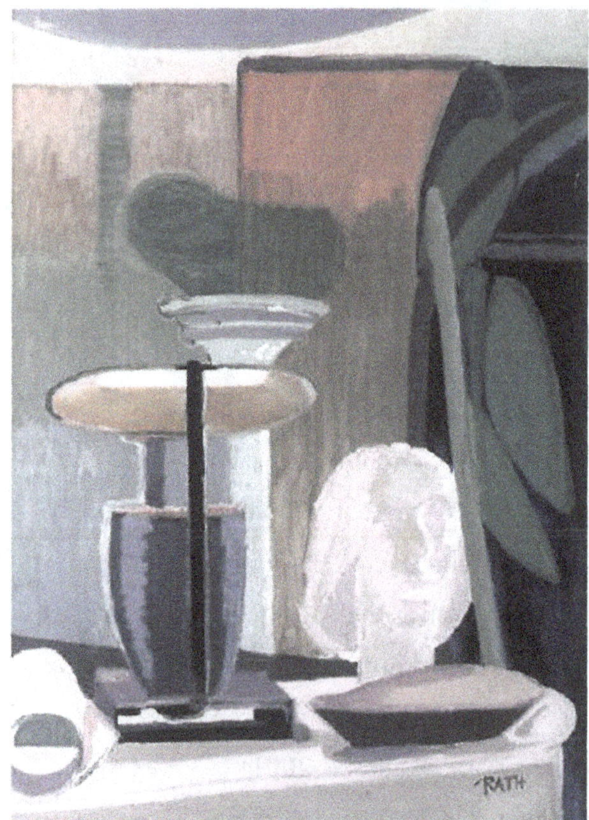

Plate 16

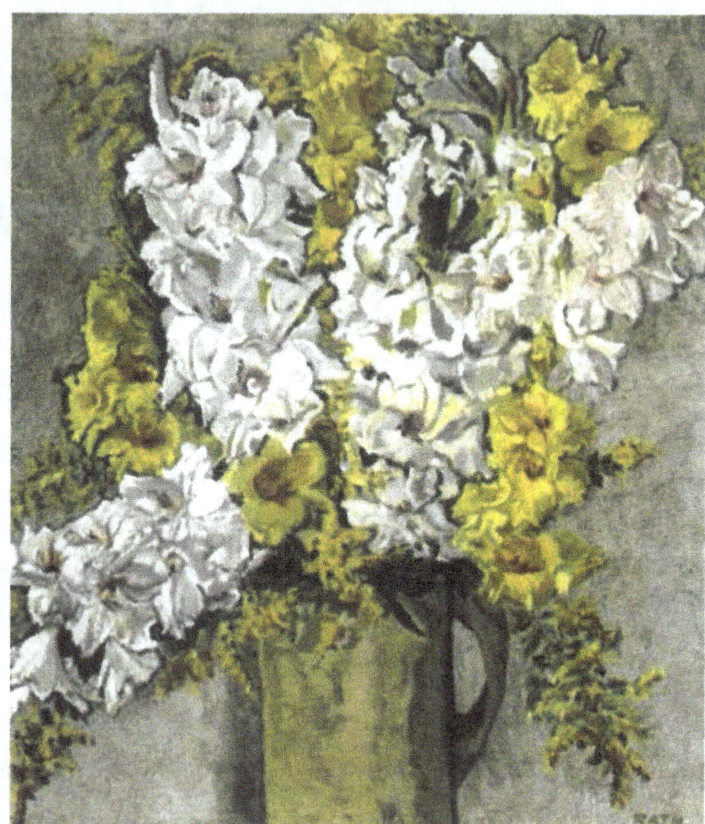

Plate 17

in the Notable Americans of the Bicentennial Era and in Marquis's *Who's Who in American Art* and she is represented in the Metropolitan Museum of Art, the New York Public Library, the Brooklyn Museum, the Library of Congress and her works can be found in over 800 public and private collections in the world.

When Rath emigrated to the USA with Gross, they initially stayed with her brothers Dolf and Walter Rath who lived in Dorset, Vermont, where they were later to purchase property. Dorset is one of a string of small villages located in a narrow valley between tree-covered mountains. Despite its remoteness, Dorset has been known among landscape painters and other artists since the turn of the last century. It began as a small artists colony, and in 1924, some of the artist-regulars banded together to sell their paintings to visitors at an exhibition which was held in Manchester, which is a few miles from Dorset. This became an annual event, and the artists became the founders of what is now the Southern Vermont Arts Center. By the time Rath and her husband arrived the Center was among the more successful regional artists' organizations in the USA (Dimond, 2007).

Rath's relations were extraordinarily creative. It is known that Walter Rath was an inventor and had been employed by a company in Nashua, New Hampshire that worked for NASA. He is credited with developing the gauge that equalized pressure in space suits so that man could walk safely on the moon — a picture of his invention used to hang on a wall in his house (Morell, 2007). Also living in the USA at that time was Paul Kollsman, Rath's uncle. He, too, was an inventor. He had studied civil engineering in Stuttgart and Munich before emigrating to the USA in 1923. His specialty was barometers and flight instruments. One of his instruments was later adopted by the NASA Apollo programme. The sensitive setting window for aircraft altimeters is still called the 'Kollsman Window'.

In 1948 and nearing retirement Paul Kollsman purchased 800 acres of land in Dorset and established the Snow Valley Ski Resort, which was formally opened in January 1942 and became one of the earliest ski areas in the USA. The nephews of Paul Kollsman, Walter and Dolf Rath, were appointed to run the resort.

On 30 July 1948, not long after their arrival in the USA, Hildegard sent a letter to the Southern Vermont Artists Inc. with an outline of her and her husband's profiles with the purpose of exploring the possibility of exhibiting their work. The letter was successful for, from 28 August to 6 September, their work was shown at the 19th Annual Exhibition of the Southern Vermont Artists which was held in Manchester, Vermont. The archives of the Southern Vermont Arts Center reveal what Hildegard Rath and Hermann Gross exhibited:

Hildegard Rath	
72 Flowers	$700
133 Notre Dame de Paris	$800
141 Wild Flowers	$600
169 The Quarry	$600
Hermann Gross	
315 The Quarry	$120
320 A Winter in Dorset	$120
368 Angelus Congregationis	$1000
393 And They Sang a New Song	$1200

In a report on the exhibition which appeared in the local newspaper the *Manchester Journal* (2 September 1948), there is reference to some big names exhibiting at the show, including "Jay Connoway, Guy Pene du Bois and the couple Hermann Gross and his wife, Hildegard Rath, the latter a sister of Walter and Dolf Rath of Snow Valley fame" (Dimond, 2007).

Rath and Gross did not settle permanently in Vermont. From 1949 to 1954 Rath was the Director of Painting at the European School of Fine Arts in New York City. This necessitated the purchase of an apartment on Fifth Avenue in New York. She painted a picture of Washington Square that was visible from their apartment. It was by no means unusual for artists to spend their summers in Vermont and return to New York for the winter. And it seems probable that they retained some accommodation in Dorset. Maintaining two residences would not have been so expensive as it is today.

It is possible that at the Southern Vermont Artists exhibition, Rath and Gross met Robert McIntyre, who was not only a summer resident but also a member of the Southern Vermont Artists. Crucially, McIntyre owned the Macbeth Gallery in New York. Some form of contact had clearly been established subsequent to the SVA Exhibition because Rath was writing to him from Dorset on 11 October 1948. In her letter she indicated that she would leave it to him to choose those paintings of her husband that he thought would be most fitting for the proposed exhibition. She also begged him to put what her husband had to say about himself in good English. Three weeks later on 1 November Rath wrote a further letter to McIntyre in which she expressed the belief that she had failed in her earlier letter to give a well rounded idea of her husband's career. She then asked if there was some way in which the exhibition could be more actively promoted. She concluded by observing that: "for our mutual interest we should greatly like to speak over what is most necessary and helpful to make his New York showing a success artistically and financially" (Kashmiry, 2007).

Prior to the exhibition, Rath enlisted the assistance of Paul Kollsman's wife — Julie Dorothea Baronin von Bodenhausen — a member of the German aristocracy. Julie Kollsman sent to McIntyre a list of her friends in New York high society who she thought might wish to attend. The letter was written from the Kollsman's permanent suite at the Waldorf Astoria in New York. Among those on the list were Princess Fahkry, Princess Boncompagni, Viscount Selby, Mrs Alice Pleydell-Bouverie (formerly Baroness Montagu of Beaulieu), Mrs Nathan Milstein, Raymond Loewy (industrial designer responsible for Shell International, Exxon, Lucky Strike cigarette package and Greyhound Bus logos and interior creative designer for Saturn I and V and Skylab) and Erling Naess, multimillionaire Norwegian shipping magnate (Kashmiry, 2007).

First Macbeth Gallery Exhibition: 1948

The Macbeth Gallery has a long and distinguished history with each successive proprietor making a significant contribution to art in America. William Macbeth, a Scots-Irish immigrant, established the Gallery in 1892. He was determined to dedicate his gallery to the permanent exhibition and sale of American pictures, both in oils and watercolours. Although some of the gallery's earliest exhibitions were of work by European artists, the business soon became the only gallery in continuous operation to keep American art permanently on display.

Robert McIntyre, a nephew of the founder, ran the Gallery in the 1940s and 1950s. Although interested in contemporary art he found that, for the most part, it did not pay. He continued operations until 1953 when he decided that doing so for profit was not only a financial burden but also ran counter to his desire to spend more time devoted to his first love — early American art. After closing his gallery's doors for the last time, he sold art from his New York apartment and from his home in Dorset, Vermont.

The brochure prepared by McIntyre for the exhibition points out that Gross was one of the many war casualties who had been forced to leave the scenes of his youth and early manhood in order to seek refuge in a free land, where there was an opportunity for him to work out in his own way the long cherished ideals of Christianity and their application to human conduct.

Gross is quoted as saying:

> Out of the nothing of the devastation of Europe, it seems to me that the Bible and its message is a salvation. There is nothing which is not

> reflected there … their symbolisms are everlasting and modern in their significance … to give form to these everlasting themes is for me a resurrection.

Caroline Wagner, who was very familiar with Gross' work, comments that many of his paintings at this time centred on the biblical scenes of the crucifixion — most of them painted in an extraordinarily impetuous style. To Wagner what is striking about these paintings is not simply the subject matter but their appearance. Because of the speedy, rough brush strokes and expressive use of colours the viewers' eyes cannot come to rest.

> "They wander among the confusingly crossed lines and the garish colours that contrast with the gloomy shades in the background. The colours mingle in the turmoil; they become softened and lose their luminosity, and thus the impasto dots and strokes finally applied by the artist at crucial points make an especially radiant impression" (Wagner, 1991).

The description of Gross in the exhibition brochure as a war casualty can be interpreted in different ways. It is certainly true that like many other refugees from war-ravaged Europe, Gross had to pick up the pieces of his life. Wagner observes that Gross' move to the United States, his unsettled married life and perhaps the delayed assimilation of his war experience precipitated a human crisis which he expressed not only in his diary entries but also in his artistic work (Wagner, 1991).

In his dark and unremittingly bleak post-war paintings Gross appears to have found a vehicle for expressing his innermost feelings. He may have felt that he had not only compromised his integrity as an artist through his involvement in Goering's propaganda unit but also betrayed the fraternity of artists, particularly those in Paris. Gross makes the point that these images represented for him a form of 'resurrection' — a personal way of exorcising the ghosts of the past and assuaging his feelings of guilt.

Second Macbeth Gallery Exhibition: 1951

There was a second exhibition of Gross' work at the Macbeth Gallery in 1951. On 5 January 1951 Gross wrote to McIntyre from 20 Fifth Avenue, New York, indicating the titles of the paintings he wanted to exhibit. The exhibition was held from 22 January to 10 February 1951. McIntyre provided the following commentary:

> In this, his second exhibition since coming to this country a few years ago, Hermann Gross is still preoccupied with the theme of Christ — His short life on earth, His death and resurrection, but above all His teachings. It is a theme deeply inwoven in his own life. Christ, to Gross, was not only a great philosopher but a great psychologist whose profound yet simple principles of the art of living have as much force and application today as in His own time. In this present era of unrest and rampant greed for power and dominion in part so much like the dark ages, Gross feels that Christianity, with all its invariable and fundamental ethical principles and precepts, is once again being crucified: that the only means of salvation the world can ever look for is through a renascence (sic) of those same old and abiding principles of moral and spiritual values. But he feels also, that in spite of this casting aside of these, the only true permanent values, we are but going through a time of trial and error: that eventually the black cumulus clouds of dissension and war, of jealousy and greed, will give way to the penetrating light of a new moral perception that this light will reach into the hearts of men, and there give birth to a new earnestness of purpose, there create a revitalised wisdom and knowledge concerning the purpose of living. And, as Gross thinks, if men will only see, will only feel the great truths of Christ's teaching, the process of healing is simple — simple as being cleansed in the water of the river Jordan. The Golden Rule is not a precept to be learned merely by rote, something vaguely useful, sentimental, to be passed lightly over, but rather an active, powerful force lacking which the world must needs be chaos. Such thoughts as these

> Gross seeks to crystallise in pictures, often of great sensuous beauty, not however giving up their content to the casual glance, communicative only to the contemplative, even reverent mind. And, as with so many of today's artists who convey their reflections concerning the present fabric of world society, its political frustrations, economic insecurity and at times forlorn hope, in non-objective form, so, too, does Gross use the language of abstract art, sometimes to the point of extreme distortion for the better emphasis of a particular thought. But at the same time, the structure of his themes is developed around objective forms which as they slowly emerge to the understanding mind become living, sentient beings, symbols, in their various attitudes, of despair, futility as in 'Crucifixion' and 'Entombment', yet, as in 'Resurrection', of faith and hope! (Kashmiry, 2007).

In the review of the Gross' second Macbeth Gallery exhibition, the art critic of *The New York Times* saw Gross as a descendant of the German Expressionist movement, where distortion and exaggeration are used for emotional effect. A feature of Expressionism which is clearly evident in Gross' work is the use of intense colour, agitated brushstrokes and disjointed space. He does not attempt to portray objective reality but rather his emotions and responses to objects and events that excite him. It is a highly subjective, personal and spontaneous form of expression. More important to Gross than achieving harmony and form was the need to achieve the highest emotional intensity so that the paintings reflect his state of mind rather than the reality of the external world. We know from his notebooks that he was influenced by the work of such Expressionists as Wassily Kandinsky, Oskar Kokoschka and George Rouault. Gross saw the purpose of art in the following terms:

> "Art, in one sense, is a quest for the unknown. Such is our experience in trying to unite colour and shape in a synthesising harmony, that then — and only then — the trace of some content arises. We always recognise the merging theme with unexpected surprise and, from then on, the content becomes of primary importance. We are at liberty to reject the character of this content, because our dignity and responsibility

> are aroused. The time of *'l'art pour l'art'* is over. Now we have to exert responsibility" (Gross, 1989).

It has been possible to identify only two of the reviewers: Alice Louchheim art critic for *The New York Times* and Carlyle Burrows art critic of the *New York Herald Tribune*. Louchheim was pre-eminent among New York art critics. She became the associate art editor and critic at *The New York Times* from 1948 to 1953 and associate art critic from 1954 to 1958. In 1954 she married the noted Finnish-born architect Eero Saarinen.

On 20 March 1951 McIntyre wrote to Gross, drawing attention to the fact that the season was drawing to a close and that he was about to start his annual spring-cleaning and part of that process involved returning pictures to artists. He indicated that he was retaining a few of his watercolours but would be obliged if arrangements could be made for the collection of the rest, as he had only limited storage space. Eight of the watercolours listed by Gross in his letter of 5 January were returned. On 14 February 1953 McIntyre wrote that as the lease on his present location was due to expire in April, he was in the process of straightening out his records and part of that involved returning as many pictures as possible to artists. He had four of Gross' watercolours that he wished to return.

Notwithstanding the commendation from one of America's foremost art critics, Gross's work appears not to have sold. This is perhaps not altogether surprising as few collectors are likely to have been overeager to hang the kind of sombre religious paintings that Gross was producing. His wife however was having more success perhaps because her subject matter was less demanding and had more instant appeal. In the eight years that he spent in the USA, he had had only two major exhibitions — both of these in the same gallery — where few of his paintings seem to have been bought.

Whilst in America Gross designed scenery and props for a number of theatrical productions including a spoken dance version of the Greek tragedy *Elektra*. A report on this production, which was published in *The Concord Monitor* (1 July 1952), singled out for particular praise "the exquisite scenery" created by Gross (The Concord Monitor, 1952). Attention was also drawn to the masks and metal headgear that Gross had both designed and made (Plates 5–6).

Some of the comments of the New York art critics on the 1948 and 1951 Macbeth Gallery Exhibitions are presented below.

New York Times: 12 December 1948
At Macbeth's Hermann Gross's religious imagery in gouache and watercolor, a cross bred of Blake and Roualt, are deeply imagined and utterly convincing within the limits of his own quite personal use of medium. And the design also carries personal conviction.

Art Digest: 15 December 1948
Hermann Gross, in his first showing in the United States at the Macbeth Gallery, creates an impression of genuine religious fervor. Not only are his watercolors and drawing concentrated on biblical themes but their content is unmistakeably inspired and directed by conviction in the message of true Christianity. Although the songs are not new they are still sung in this instance with unrestricted vigor and unrelenting accent on the ethical tones.

New York Herald Tribune: 19 December 1948
Hermann Gross is showing a group of recent watercolors and drawings at the Macbeth gallery through this month. His watercolors are rather murky and imbued with a religious if somewhat abstruse air, but they do make a strong appeal to the emotions, and in "*Gesmas — The Malefactor to the Right of Christ and Crucifixion* he has reached his climax. His drawings are heavy but sometimes come close to profundity, particularly his rendering of *The Malefactor to the Left of Christ.*

Art News: December 1948
His work, forbidden and branded as degenerate by the Nazis, has passed through the crucible of war-torn Europe and shows in a group of forceful, haunting compositions in watercolor and crayon, the regeneration of deep artistic and moral convictions. His favorite themes are inspired

by the Bible, from which he extracts images that run the gamut from a powerful expressionism to geometrically organized abstractions.

The Sun: 19 December 1948

The Hermann Gross drawings in the Macbeth Gallery are exceedingly somber and somewhat confused but if anybody has a right to be somber and confused it is Mr Gross for he is one of the displaced artists from Germany obliged to start a new career in a new land. He is religious, occupying himself with themes from many angles but not arriving, on the present occasion, at any very satisfactory compositions. He has a leaning toward the abstract, and the most moving of his compositions is the most abstract of all, the one called *The Malefactor to the Left of Christ*, and in it there is a shaft of light penetrating the darkness which must be allowed to be dramatic.

The New York Times: 26 January 1951

His watercolors now at the Macbeth Gallery use both abstraction and stylisation as means of expression for his religious subjects. Perhaps his greatest gift is a mastery of smoldering and effective color, patches of which get put together like a fluid changing mosaic. Obviously a descendant of the German Expressionists, Gross makes personal use of these idioms. Here is religious painting in a wholly contemporary mode, weakened neither by sentimentality nor adherence to worn-out imagery. The implications reach out into twentieth-century living. Curiously, the more abstract of these paintings seem to have the clearest and most forceful impact.

New York Herald Tribune: 28 January 1951

Of two artists exhibiting figurative work, Hermann Gross at the Macbeth gallery is the more dramatic in his paintings of religious subjects. Here, the atmosphere of the show is heavy with movement, the dark and shattered surfaces of the canvasses giving impressions reminiscent of Kokoschka and German Expressionists.

Pictures on Exhibition: February 1951

Hermann Gross's watercolors at the Macbeth Gallery are truly inspirational. Never has the story of Christ been told with deeper humility, with greater reverence or with more exalted joyousness. There is nothing literary about Mr Gross's paintings. Just a suggestion of a figure or figures appear in *Under the Cross*, *The Resurrection* and *Entombment* but those figures combined with glorious color carry as much spiritual uplift as the written word.

Art Digest: February 1951

His watercolors in this exhibition, tending toward an abstraction and distortion of form make a brilliantly emphatic collection built around a single tempera painting *The Descent from the Cross*. Often mystic in his conception, as in *The Inspiration*, Gross shows hints of a rugged realism buried deep behind many of his more abstract watercolors, as in *Touch Me Not*, and the fine, fluid *Jacob's Dream*, and the painting of *Abraham Tempted To Offer Isaac for Sacrifice*, with its brilliantly suggestive form, emergent from the brilliantly rich color.

Art News: February 1951

Gross, a Stuttgart-born artist, branded as degenerate by the Nazis, whose trend towards semi-abstract religious painting was already noted here in 1948, is more expressionist than geometric in the watercolors, as if the idea rather than the visual elements had dominated.

7. 1956–1963: Germany

Gross never quite succeeded in adjusting to America and that adventure ended in failure. On returning to Germany, Gross turned up at the home of his friend Hans Haustein in Stuttgart. He had lost hope and confidence. Not only was he not selling his art in the USA but also his marriage was disintegrating. Haustein wondered how he could help. He then remembered Trude Sand, a journalist who had been a member of Gross' circle of friends in Berlin. By chance Haustein had recently heard her when one of her programmes for children had been broadcast by Radio Stuttgart. He found her telephone number and invited her to come round and see Gross. Haustein was convinced that this meeting would prove to be immensely important (Haustein, 1991). And so it proved. Gross did not return to New York. He and Trude Sand rented a studio together. They both continued to work independently and then they moved in together. As soon as the divorce certificate from the USA arrived, they married.

In 1956 Gross had an exhibition of his work in the Town House in Freudenstadt. A review of the exhibition in the *Schwarzwaldzeitung* for 26 November 1956 refers to an earlier exhibition in Freudenstadt in 1946 when Gross had displayed sculptures and artwork which had astonished visitors because of the diversity of the work exhibited. The review went on to comment that the subtlety and delicacy of the sculptures and charcoal drawings conveyed the impact of war and the post war period. It was noted that Gross had remained faithful to his mission and had not moved away from his earlier vision. All the exhibits demonstrated intense empathy and experience and involved deep concerns and the expression of Christian faith. The reviewer noted that at the beginning of the Advent season it was a delightful thought that there was still a contemporary artist who saw his mission in creating artwork based on religious themes.

A review in the *Schwarzwald Bote* for the 26 November drew particular attention to a work that Gross described as *Doppelgesicht* (Double Face). The face of a young woman had been hammered out of a thin iron sheet. When the viewer looks at the reverse side, the faces on both sides appear to be separated by millennia. The work is presented not simply as a technical experiment but a questioning as to the meaning of outward appearance.

After Freudenstadt the exhibition moved to the Galerie Wasmuth in Berlin. A review for the *Telegraf* on 13 January 1957 observed that some of his paintings resembled stained glass windows and gave the impression of serene solemnity. The colours and shapes were thought to be typical of early German Expressionist artists. A further review, which appeared in the Berlin newspaper *Der Kurier* on the 13 January, was entitled 'Mystische Versponnenheit' (Mystical Eccentricity)! The reviewer concluded that the works exhibited — paintings, sculptures and designs — bore the hallmark of a visionary poet who was able to create work of an unorthodox but exciting nature.

We are given an insight into Gross' thinking about the character and purpose of art in the outline of an address he gave at the opening of an exhibition of his work at the Mescher Studio in Stuttgart on 30 September 1962. In his opinion, the conventional form for exhibitions tended to set apart the work of the artists, who are like shadowy figures in the background, from the viewers. The so-called authorities that comment upon and evaluate the work exhibited often, through their writing, transform artists into heroes, especially if they (i.e., the artists) are dead! If one wants to learn something about an artist — a man who is neither a shadowy background figure still less a hero — then, Gross suggests, speak directly to him. As to any judgement of the value of his own work, as far as he can pass critical comment upon it, such judgement takes place constantly. As to the judgement of other people, Gross felt it was often too subjective. It told him more about the viewer than the work itself. In his opinion, such judgements must, like their creators, have time to mature. However one should not remain quiet. Gross argued that we need to talk and bridge the chasm that divides artists from non-artists. This was a matter of particular concern to Gross. In genuine art, Gross argued, something lives that cannot be grasped. Through artistic effort a spark may be ignited that is all too quickly extinguished. We need to continue the search, until we find that spark again. It was the spark which was the only reality for Gross. Whether it was present in his own work, Gross did not know (Gross 1962).

8. 1963–1988: Scotland

In 1963, to the total bewilderment of all his friends, Gross decided to leave Stuttgart and move to Scotland. Marjorie Rosenthal, a friend of Gross, recalled having a meeting in Stuttgart with Trude Sand in which Trude had told her that she had met a friend who was actively involved in some capacity with the Waldorf School in the city, and who had expressed great interest in the metal work that Gross had created in his early years. It was this friend who subsequently told Dr Karl König, co-founder of the Camphill Movement, about Gross (Rosenthal, 1989). After some time had elapsed a meeting was arranged between König and Gross which took place on the shores of Lake Zürich. König was very impressed by Gross' personality and his evident craftsmanship and invited him to come to Scotland. So early in 1962 Gross and his wife made their first visit to Camphill. Gross gave a talk and showed slides of his work in the chapel at Newton Dee, a Camphill community on the outskirts of Aberdeen. 1962 is an important date in one other respect, for it witnessed the opening of Camphill Hall in the grounds of the Camphill Rudolf Steiner School. The intention was that the Hall should become the spiritual home of the Camphill Movement. König clearly had Gross in mind for the construction of a number of metal sculptures for the Hall depicting the *Archangels Michael and Raphael* and *A Praying Man*. König imposed one condition which was that the work had to be undertaken within Camphill, for, in König's opinion, if it were carried out elsewhere, it would lack meaning and authenticity (Plates 18–20).

Gross' move to Scotland may be seen in the context of the profound influence on modern art of the writings of not only Henri Bergson, Sigmund Freud and Friedrich Nietzsche but also Rudolf Steiner (Acton, 2004). Wassily Kandinsky in *Concerning the Spiritual in Art*, refers to Steiner's interest in providing alternative means of spiritual communication given that religion had been so fundamentally questioned (Kandinsky, 1979). Kandinsky was particularly concerned to make contact with what lay beneath the surface and the inner feelings of the spectator. Steiner contended that it was possible to encounter this divine

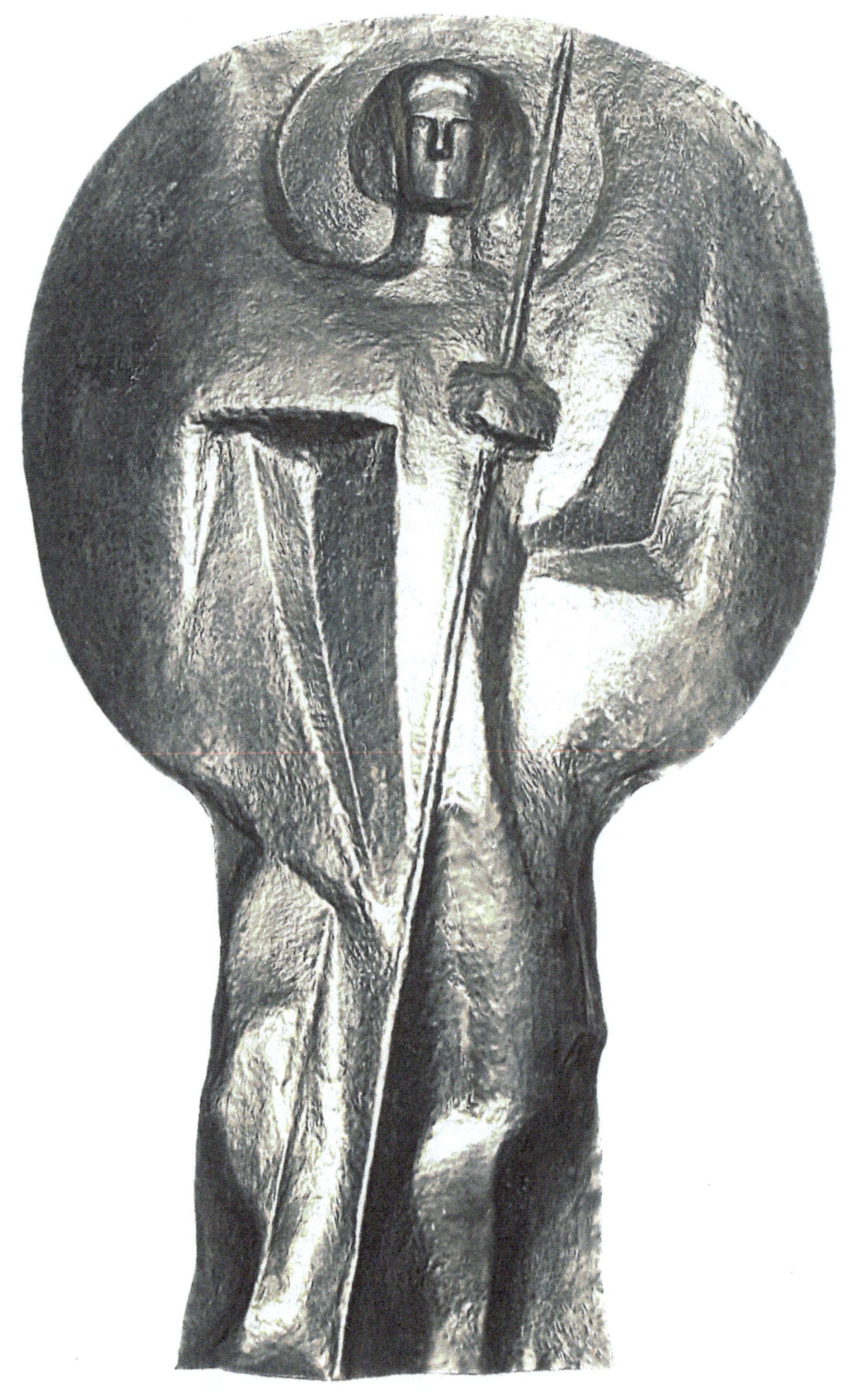

Plate 18

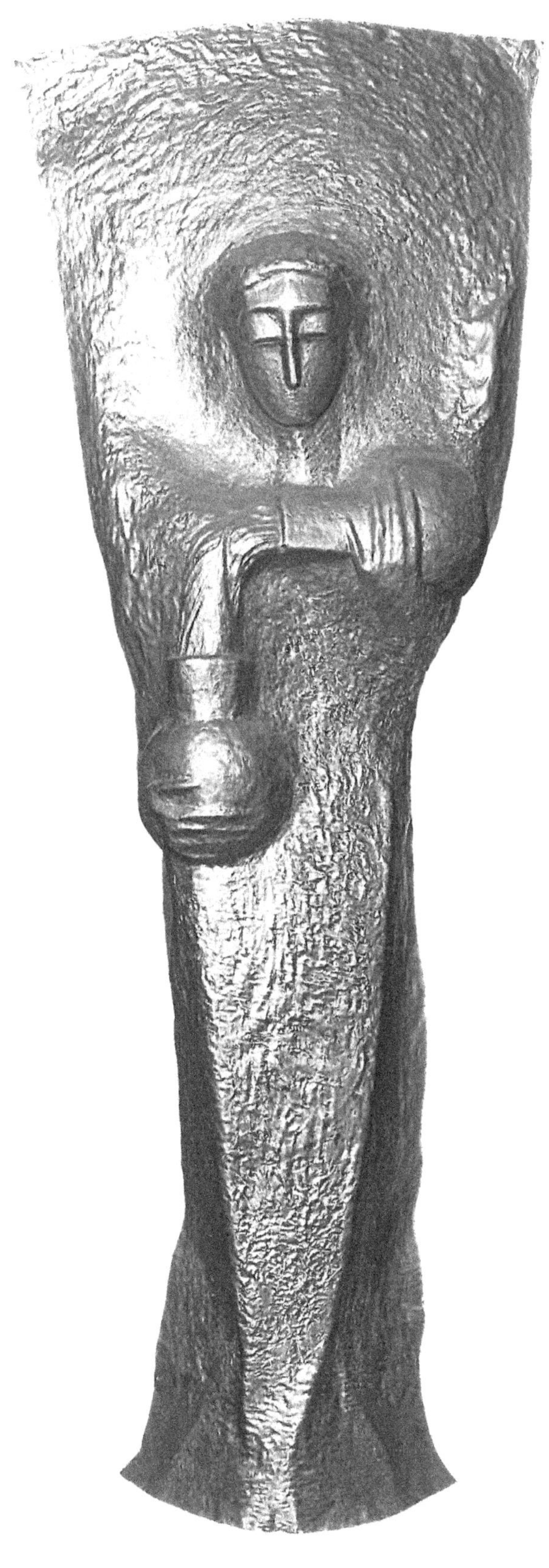

Plate 19

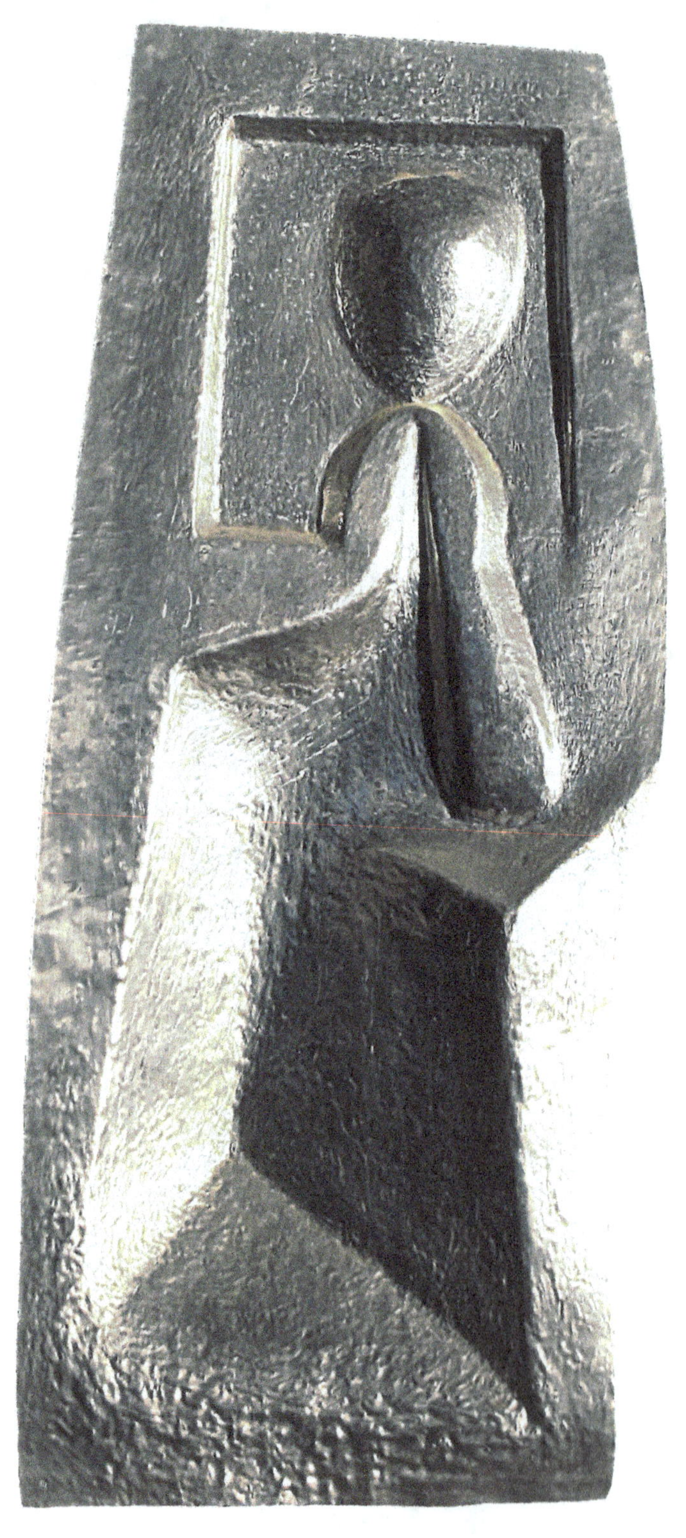

Plate 20

or spiritual dimension behind the world of appearances. It was necessary to form inner 'images charged with content' and without recourse to the sense impressions of real objects. One needed to learn to think in images, even when there was no object to arouse one's senses. Over time Kandinsky developed an ability to conceive of pictorial forms in purely abstract terms (Ringborn, 1985). As they stood on the shore of Lake Zürich, König and Gross would have shared a common language both recognising and valuing the spiritual dimension in art and seeking ways to give artistic expression to the human spirit.

Gross was aware that moving to Scotland would mean abandoning home and friends, beginning a new life in a strange country at an age when most people could not bear to be uprooted. It was above all a deep spiritual decision that he would live *for* art rather than *from* it: that he would give and not take (Dunbar, 1963). Thus the time spent living and working in a Camphill community was the last chapter in Gross' biography.

Camphill

König and a group of refugees from Austria and Germany had founded the Camphill communities at the beginning of World War II. König had developed a vision of a 'learning community' where the traditional boundaries between professional disciplines would be dissolved; where the spiritual well-being of those living in the community would be nurtured and respected; where creativity, spontaneity and originality would be encouraged; and, where ecological sensitivity and responsibility would be exercised. He was looking at one possible way to generate social renewal at a time of social disintegration and to send a message of hope at a time of widespread despair (Jackson, 2006). Having experienced some of the horrors of a hate-fuelled Nazi regime, König was determined to create a community in which compassion and tolerance were present, for it was compassion and tolerance that bound communities together. It was König's belief that co-workers in the communities should live and work together with children and adults with special needs in such a way that new social forms might develop: the co-workers would share every aspect of their lives with the children and would work without remuneration.

Hermann Gross: man and teacher

It was within this distinctive community that Gross lived as artist-in-residence. Working in this setting became a source of inspiration to him and those who lived there. Both for the founders of Camphill and for Gross, the search for new social forms was never an abstract idea — it was an urgent necessity. As the community gave his work new life, so he offered new life to the community. It had always been one of the aims of the founders of Camphill to foster social art. Gross began a process whereby people were challenged to look at their surroundings in a new way. This stimulated an interest in what was put on the walls of the houses and meeting rooms, and in the gardens (Ravetz, 1991). Gross made a significant contribution to the community's understanding of the purpose and value of art, not simply by making his work available to the community, but by ensuring that the art-making process itself was accessible and visible and not some precious and exclusive activity. In essence, he was engaged in the demystification of the process — but not of the product.

Elizabeth and Peter Howe, friends of Gross, have commented that to live for a few years surrounded by paintings by Gross had been a 'path of learning', a continual training of the eye and the imagination. A picture which appeared difficult, even grim at first sight, gradually unfolded and revealed itself over the weeks, months and years. After seeing the same picture daily for such long periods, suddenly one day a new figure appeared, or a new colour, and with it a whole new perspective opened up. Thus, the viewer became an active participant, a co-creator. Slowly one learned that liking or disliking was irrelevant, what was important was the struggle towards meaning (Howe, 1988).

Gisela Schlegel, who came to know Gross in his final years at Camphill, observed that in inviting him to Camphill König knew that his art would not only be highly valued but would change the community (Schlegel, 1999). What particularly impressed Schlegel was the nature of the encounter of Gross with the child with a disability:

"I think this encounter very fundamentally changed his art. When he portrayed a child … we were allowed to live with his picture for some time, we valued that Hermann had seen something in the handicapped child which was deep and far beyond the everyday encounter. We, through his experience, were allowed to live then with his art in connection with such a child."

In thinking of Gross, Schlegel was reminded of the words of Pablo Casals who said of himself: "First I am a man, a human being, and then I am an artist." Schlegel acknowledged that Gross had opened up for those living in Camphill an understanding of how to look at and interpret modern art. Marianne Sander, a Camphill co-worker, has commented that many of Gross' paintings, which were to be found in the houses of Camphill communities became the daily, beloved companions of the children and co-workers alike and helped to ennoble, educate and enrich those who lived with them (Sander, 1988).

In the opinion of Volker Gebhard, a pupil of Gross, besides being a master artist, Gross was also a great teacher. When speaking of him, Gebhard suggested that one should set firmly to one side any notion of the 'artist in his ivory tower'. No trouble was too great for him. This was reflected in the concern and care shown to the children with disabilities and their carers amongst whom he lived. What he daily encountered informed many of his paintings. A fresh, honest light was shone on that distressful and artificial divide that separates the so-called psychically or bodily healthy from those less fortunate. Gebhard sensed, largely through his meeting and working with Gross, that his art had a more profound, potent and human character than is commonly supposed but one which was nevertheless attainable (Gebhard, 1988).

According to Gebhard it was impossible on entering Gross' studio to miss the aura of living orderliness and creative energy:

"... laid out in proper array were the much cared for tools, and the materials, which seemed only to wait the Master — who would surely be along any moment now — to burst into a song of delight about the undying reign of colour and shape. Here too was a wordless but utterly clear message about the discipline of hard work born of a dedicated, open heart."

Peter Schirmer noted that, as a teacher, Gross was precise and unorthodox (Schirmer, 1991). He tried to pass on the essence of his own approach and it was the responsibility of the students then to proceed further with their own observations and experiences. Gross made high demands both on himself and on his students. He believed that each artist, provided he is true to himself, was aware of the continuous tendency toward cliché, for creative art produces both genuine and clichéd art. Gross sought to train the student's sensitivity to detect and discriminate between such tendencies in their own work. He insisted that every attempt in creating art demanded a total commitment of all the means at the artist's disposal. It was of less importance to him whether one's attempt succeeded or failed. More important for the artist was the opportunity to experiment and to learn from the experience.

Gross placed great value on craftsmanship and the fact that there were rules in every craft that cannot be ignored by a serious student of art. Crafts were the base from which one started and returned to whenever one reached a dead-end whether in painting or sculpting. Whilst Gross accepted tradition in art, he was not in awe of it. Each work he undertook opened up a new realm of aesthetic and ethical possibilities.

Marga Schnell, a pupil of Gross, recollected her fond memories of working with him. She remembered that when she went to visit him, she was first greeted with Turkish coffee and then offered his special chair to sit in. She was treated as an important person. Schnell noted that Gross was very sparing with his words: one met him through his pictures. When, with great ceremony, he put a painting up on his easel, there would be a silence but a filled silence. Characteristically, he never gave a title to any of his paintings. He said very little, being much more interested in the observations of the viewer. He would be very amused when something was seen in the painting that he had not perhaps intended. Schnell observed that Gross not only brought art to Camphill but also his quality of looking beyond what one sees — a legacy that has remained in Camphill. By guiding his students in this way, Gross opened a new world to each one. Not only did abstract art become accessible but also nature suddenly revealed itself in a new light (Schnell, 1989).

Stefan Geider, another pupil of Gross, recalled the many occasions that he had sat with Gross in the evening, eating cheese and baguettes accompanied by a glass of French red wine. It was a time when Gross shared some of his intimate memories of the past. On one occasion he described the circumstances surrounding his time in Paris — a city which because of its creative atmosphere acted as a magnet for so many artists. He spoke of his many personal encounters and relationships, his highs and lows and his search for artistic truth and freedom. Like so many other artists Gross was very poor. He lived from day to day, making money where he could, the rest of his time was spent painting, sculpting and drawing. Because of his great talent for drawing, he found many jobs, some legal and some illegal, copying papers, designs and even, on occasion, passports! (Geider, 2008).

On a few rare occasions he talked of the time that he had studied and worked along with a few other art students in Picasso's studio. Gross had greatly admired Picasso both for his humanity and his art. It was for Gross the most important and formative time in his life to be in the presence of Picasso. He felt that his inner being was being addressed and many unknown qualities in his being were awakened. His greatest disappointment and pain was experienced when one of the students so upset Picasso that he threw them out of his studio and did not allow them to return. However a short time later Picasso did allow Gross to see him again. At this meeting Picasso took a large blank piece of paper and wrote his signature at the bottom. He then told Gross that if he was ever in real despair, he could fill the paper and make use of it in whatever way he thought fit. For Gross this was the greatest present that he had ever received, for it showed Picasso's trust in his moral character and acknowledged his professionalism. He treasured the paper for the rest of his life and never had cause to use it (Geider, 2008). Catherine Imhof-Cardinal, one of Gross' pupils, remembered him telling her that when he was stationed in Paris during the war, he went to see Picasso. As he entered the studio, he became aware of the fact that he was wearing his German Air Force uniform — in other words of his being the enemy — and he had apologised profusely. However, Picasso had very graciously brushed the apology aside and had simply said: "I only see the painter in you" (Imhof-Cardinal, 2008).

9. Themes

We have noted that in the immediate aftermath of the war, Gross' paintings were explicitly religious in content and were acknowledged by him to represent a working out of his own inner emotional and spiritual turmoil. With the passage of time and particularly from the moment he assumed the role of artist-in-residence in Camphill the character of his work underwent a significant change. The two themes of 'masks and masquerades' and 'children in care' to which attention will be drawn pose questions about identity and mission: 'Who am I?' and 'What is my purpose?' It is difficult to think of two more fundamental questions for anyone to consider. Long before the notion of 'the reflective practitioner' became part of common professional parlance, Camphill co-workers had been constantly encouraged to engage in professional reappraisal and spiritual reflection. Thus, they were likely to be attuned to the messages that Gross was seeking to communicate. Whilst Gross may have had a target audience in mind, the content of his paintings has universal relevance and value.

Whilst it is not the purpose of this monograph to offer an extended critique of Gross' work, it is nevertheless important to comment on some of its features and to identify some of the key themes that emerge. The geometric construction, the restricted and understated palette owe a debt to Braque, whilst the dream-like and mythic quality of many of his other paintings remind one of Chagall. That is no surprise given that both Braque and Chagall were active in Paris at the time Gross was living and working there. However, it would be wrong to conclude that Gross was in any way a derivative artist; he clearly imposed his own quite distinctive mark on his work.

Gross made clear that he did not consciously set out to paint in an abstract manner. He sought to simplify the connections between the various elements of a picture and then slowly crystallise them into their simplest form. He would then search in that abstract form for the subject that lay dormant there. He might see a head and then, only then, would he put in a symbol for it. For Gross this was the critical moment. He then gradually progressed from the abstract construction of the coloured areas and lines to the creation of a face. Gross constantly questioned his own methods: in particular the way in which different colours could be employed, their interaction with each other as well as within the total structure of the work.

There is an interesting parallel in the approach to painting found in the work of Kandinsky and Gross. A significant number of Kandinsky's paintings are titled 'Improvisations'. In other words, they were created spontaneously or without any preparation. The paintings of Gross convey the impression that they, too, are extemporisations which start from a geometric or abstract base. While Kandinsky in his earlier paintings moved from objective reality to abstraction, Gross appears to move in the opposite direction from initial abstraction to dimly recognisable object. Kandinsky came to an appreciation of the abstract in art almost by accident. Seeing a painting of his own, lying on its side on the easel one evening, he had been struck by its beauty, a beauty beyond what he saw when he set it upright. It was the liberated colour, the formal independence, that so entranced him. In discussing the work of Kandinsky, Nicolas Pioch, art historian, has observed:

"The only meaning to be found lies in what the experience of the picture provides, and that demands prolonged contemplation. What some find hard about abstract art is the very demanding, time-consuming labour that is implicitly required. Yet if we do not look long and with an open heart, we shall see nothing but superior wallpaper" (Pioch, 2002).

Religious works

It has already been noted that religious subjects featured prominently in Gross' work in the immediate aftermath of the war. In Plate 21 we have a representation by Gross of the four creatures of the Apocalypse described in The *Book of Revelation*, Chapter 4, Verse 9:

> "And the first beast was like a lion, and the second beast like a calf, and the third beast had a face as a man, and the fourth beast was like a flying eagle."

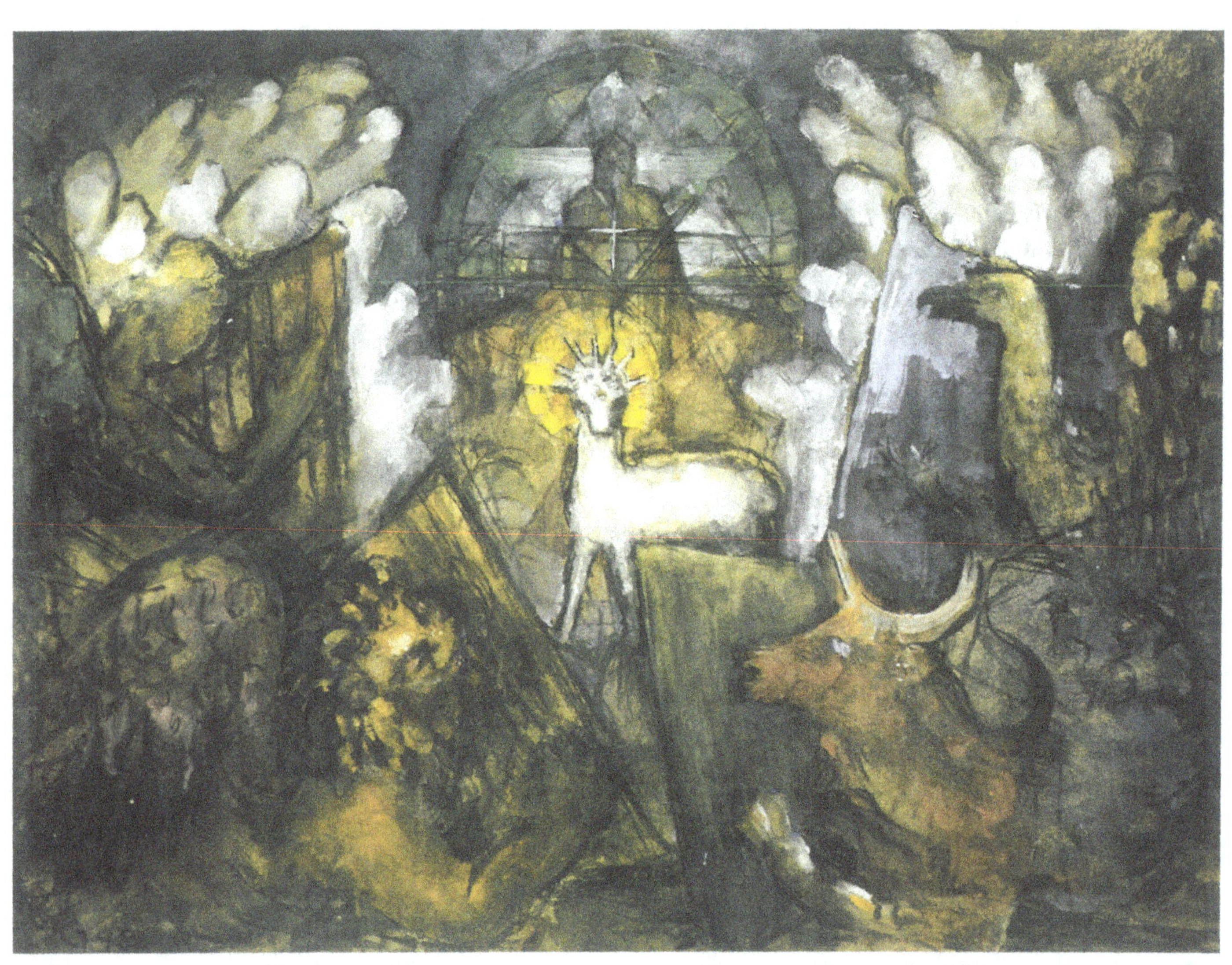

Plate 21

Mirroring the biblical text, on either side of God's throne, there are twelve elders who are clad in white raiment and wear gold crowns. Gross appears to have given a reasonably faithful representation of the scene depicted in *The Book of Revelation*. The Lamb, as here, is frequently depicted with a nimbus or halo, signifying Jesus Christ. One intriguing aspect of the painting is the representation of God in what seems like a Buddha-like pose. Is this intentional or accidental? Support for the view that it is intentional comes from the fact that in one of Gross' sketch books there is a drawing of Buddha set against a similar geometric backdrop to that shown in the painting.

It is known that this particular painting made a profound impression upon Karl König when he first saw it. This was probably when Gross and Trude Sand made their first visit to Aberdeen in 1962. The central positioning of the Lamb would have struck a chord with König given his Christocentric approach to Christianity. It may have had a further appeal given the close historical link between the Camphill Movement and the Moravian Church, whose symbol is the Lamb of God holding a banner (Jackson, 2008). It has been suggested that it was this painting that convinced König that Gross was the right person to undertake the artistic work in the Camphill Hall (Schnell, 2008). A further feature of the painting that is likely to have appealed to König is its apparent fusion of eastern and western mysticism which is a characteristic feature of anthroposophy. The symbolic significance of this painting in Camphill history is highlighted by the fact that it continues to hang in the foyer outside the entrance doors to Camphill Hall, where Gross was to create the aluminium statues (Plates 18–20) and the stained glass windows (Plates 39–41).

The fact that this painting was completed in 1948 is of interest. From 1946 to 1948 Gross was living in Paris. In 1947 there was a major retrospective of the work of Marc Chagall at the Musée National d'Art Moderne in Paris (Baal-Teshuva, 2003). It seems likely that Gross visited this exhibition and demonstrated the influence of Chagall in this composition, which is reminiscent of the kind of poetic vision encountered in Chagall's paintings.

The subject of Plate 22 is Abraham obeying God's command to sacrifice his son Isaac. This refers to the biblical story where Abraham in wishing to prove that there was only one god indicated that he was willing to do anything to show

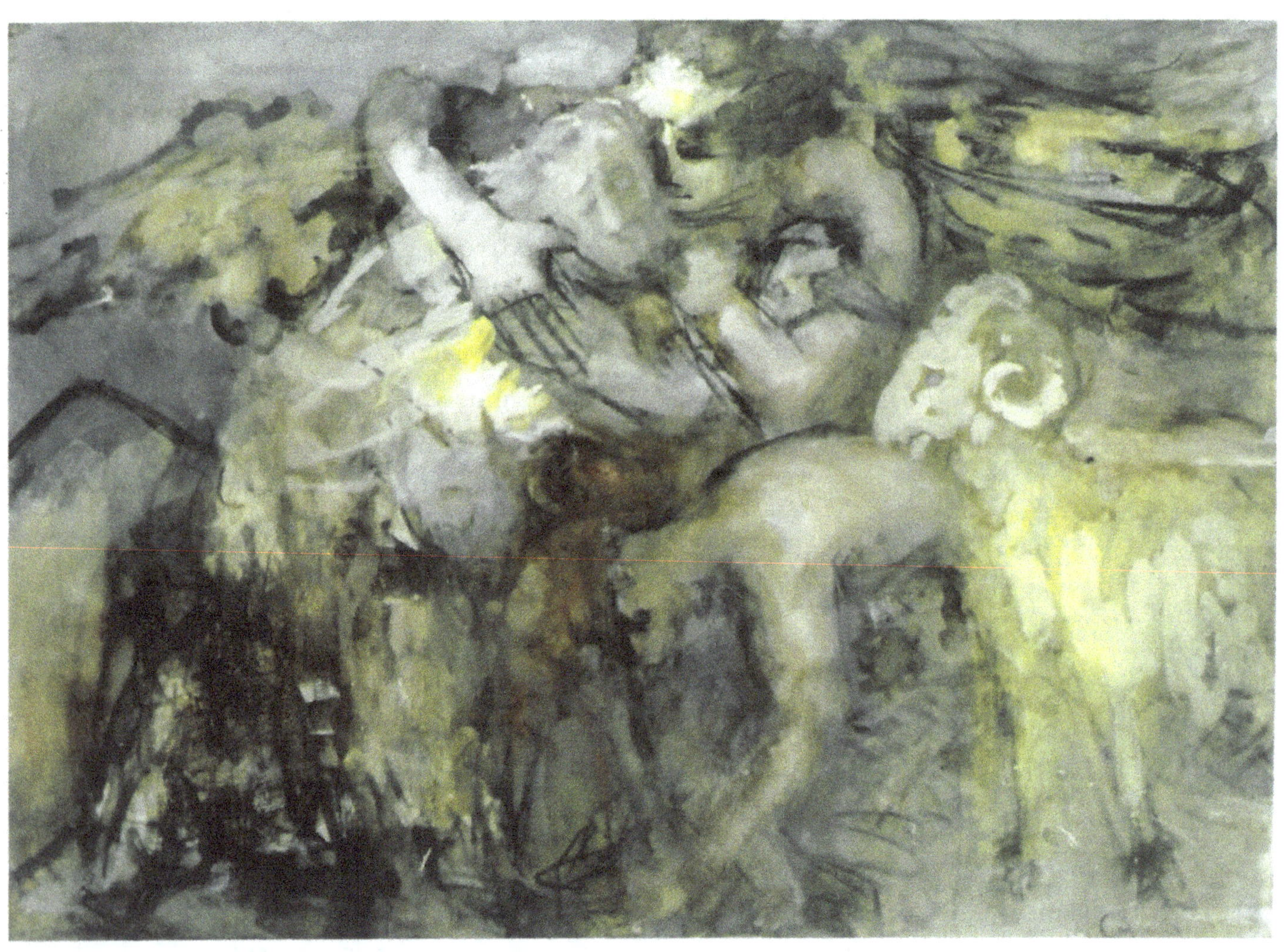

Plate 22

his devotion. So God told Abraham to go to the top of a mountain and sacrifice his son, Isaac. As Abraham was on the point of cutting his son's throat, God told him to stop. It is instructive to contrast the way in which Rembrandt and Caravaggio portray this scene with that of Gross. The painting by Rembrandt dramatically illustrates the story of the faith of Abraham (1635, Hermitage, St Petersburg). In the painting an angel is shown grasping Abraham's right hand with such force that he drops the knife. What is discomfiting for the viewer is the sight of Abraham's left hand firmly covering the whole of Isaac's face — mouth and nose — which would have had the effect of asphyxiating him. It is also clear that Isaac's hands have been tied behind his back so that he cannot resist. Caravaggio went beyond both biblical and iconographical tradition in his representation of this scene by showing an unsubmissive Isaac screaming in horror when gripped in the neck and face by his father (1603, Uffizi Gallery, Florence). It is a picture of hideous and vicious brutality with strong overtones of the sadomasochism found in Caravaggio's paintings. The painting of this theme by Gross could not be more different. Here the interceding angel holds Abraham compassionately in its arms. The gentle and soft colours used by Gross express feelings of great tenderness and concern. Abraham is depicted as a distraught and bewildered old man for whom the viewer is likely to feel more sympathy than for the Abraham depicted by Rembrandt and Caravaggio.

It is difficult to think of a starker contrast with the representation of *Abraham Tempted to offer Isaac for Sacrifice* than the portrayal of one of the malefactors crucified with Christ (Plate 23). This was one of a series of paintings of the crucifixion scene. The New York art critics were in unanimous agreement that Gross's crucifixion paintings made a profound visual and emotional impact. Some of the critics were impressed by the unrestrained vigour with which the paintings had been created. These are powerfully dramatic compositions which haunt the imagination. Aline Louchheim, the art critic of *The New York Times*, noted that paintings, such as the one illustrated in Plate 23, betrayed no sentimentality neither did they employ any hackneyed or clichéd religious imagery. These were religious paintings appropriate for the 20th century. The physical agony shown here has none of the indulgent and sensational character to be found in Caravaggio's portrayal of Isaac's suffering.

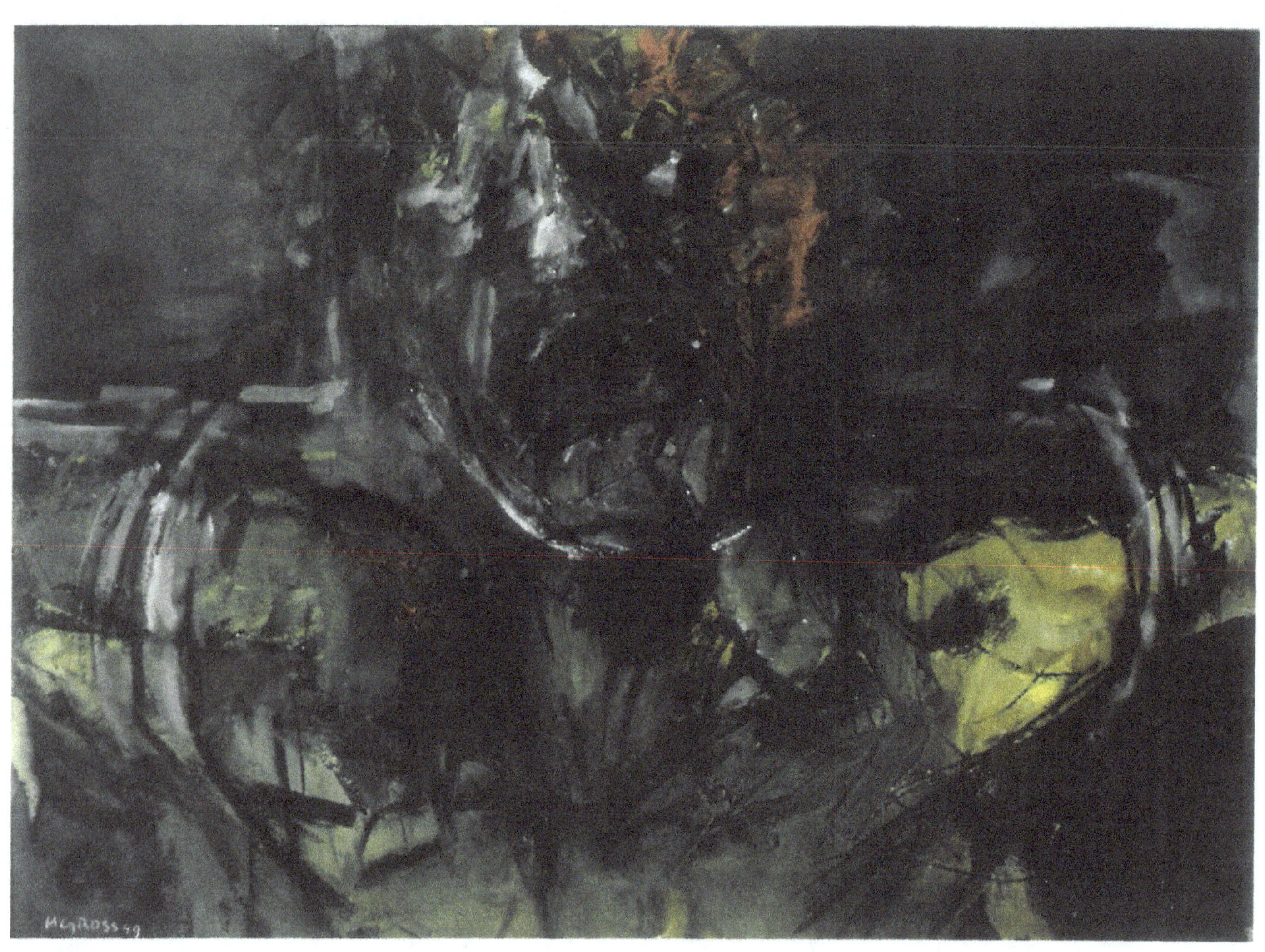

Plate 23

The impression gained from examining the way in which the paint has been applied is that Gross painted with great speed and energy and without inhibition. I am indebted to Scott Dimond for pointing out that Gross' religious work would have been seen as very 'modern' in the USA and certainly daring for a painter of traditional Christian themes. This may help explain why Gross had such trouble in selling his work: those who liked 'modern' art did not want religious paintings and those who liked appealing pictures of Jesus were not favourably disposed to modern art (Dimond, 2008).

The manner in which the paint is energetically and spontaneously applied immediately conveys the urgency on the part of the painter to give free expression to his deeply held convictions. Thus the viewer is affected both by the composition itself and the manner in which it has been produced. There is a sense in which the living process whereby this painting has been created is as important as the product.

Plate 24 shows a religious sculpture that Gross made in 1948 probably when he was in the USA. The stoup is likely to have been made to order, although who commissioned it and where it is now located is not known. A stoup is a basin for holy water found at the entrance to Roman Catholic and high Episcopalian churches. Those entering and leaving the church dip their fingers in the stoup and make the sign of the cross as a way of affirming their baptism. In this particular instance it may be a representation of the Virgin Mary who is holding the stoup. Stoups are usually unobtrusive, often located in recesses in church walls but here the person visiting the church, whether for private prayer or a service appears to come into more direct contact with the Virgin Mary. What Gross has succeeded in doing here is linking the process of personal purification through the dipping of one's fingers in the holy water with a physical representation of the embodiment of purity — the Virgin Mary. So what may conventionally be a ritual reflex for church attenders gains the potential to become more personal and meaningful.

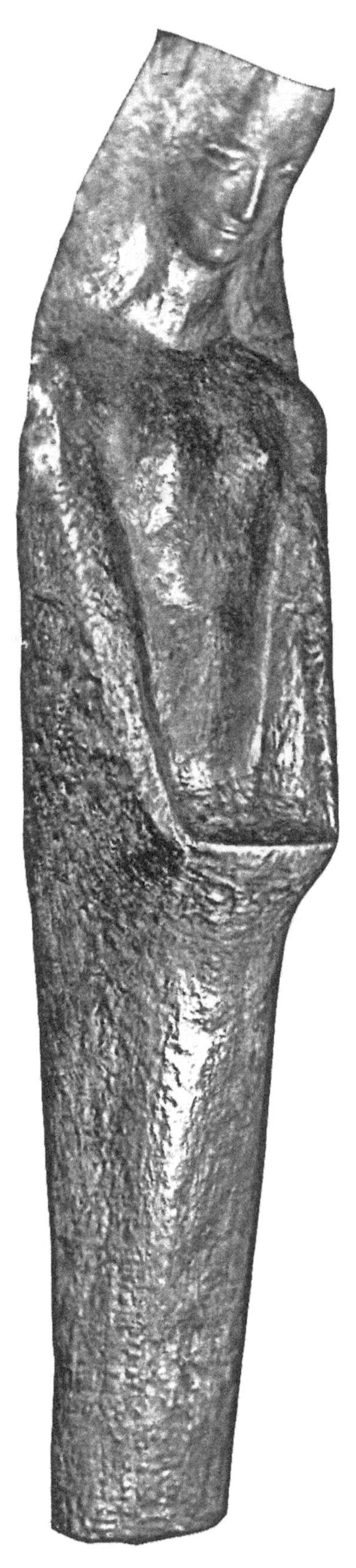

Plate 24

Masks and masquerades

Masks are a recurrent theme throughout Gross' life. We have Hans Haustein making reference to the mask behind which the young Gross danced in his parents' apartment. We have the newspaper photograph of Gross as a dancer with the *Traumbühne Schertel* in which he is wearing a mask. Then we have the black and white photographs taken by Haustein of Gross in Berlin showing him in his metal workshop constructing masks (Plates 2–4) and, finally, the photograph of the stage performance of *Elektra* in which masks made by Gross are clearly in evidence. (Plate 6)

What purpose does the mask perform? And what is its role in modern art? Most societies have used masks for various purposes. A mask hides and protects the wearer and in primitive societies it was meant to protect whoever was wearing it from spirits and evil creatures. It also transforms and endows the wearer with the strength and power of what it represents, thus making them no longer human. The mask, which is worn over or in front of the face, hides the identity of a person and by its own features, establishes another being. This essential characteristic of hiding and revealing personalities or moods is common to all masks.

A related theme that runs through the work of many Post Impressionists — Cézanne, Derain and Picasso — was carnival/masquerade and the figures of Harlequin and Pierrot, traditional figures in the ancient Commedia dell'Arte. Harlequin with his multi-coloured diamond-patterned costume, black trifold Napoleon hat is usually seen as the representation of life, its many-sidedness and riches, whilst lonely and melancholic Pierrot with his sorrowful and whitened face, white broad brimmed conical hat and white loose pyjamas hanging on him like a shroud, symbolises death. Both Harlequin and Pierrot may be depicted wearing masks or unmasked. It has been argued that Harlequin was Picasso's 'alter ego' for many years throughout his long career. Picasso appears to have identified with Harlequin's life as an individual destined to live 'outside' mainstream society. Harlequin's ability to transform whatever he touched with his magic wand suggests a metaphor for artistic creation through the use of the painter's brush.

Within the visual arts, a shift occurred that fundamentally changed the way man was depicted. In the late 1800s, Impressionist artists placed a great deal of emphasis

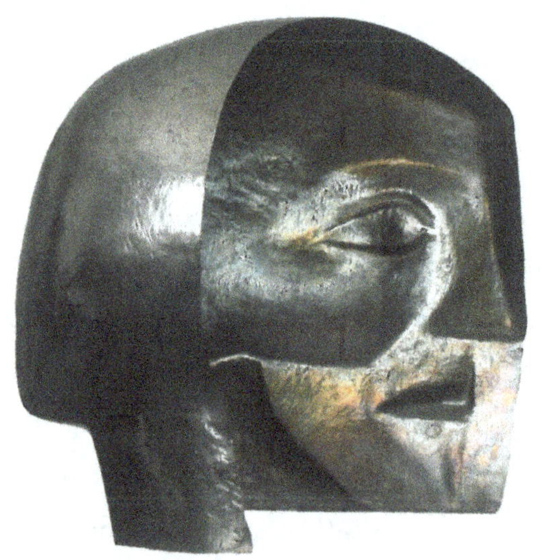

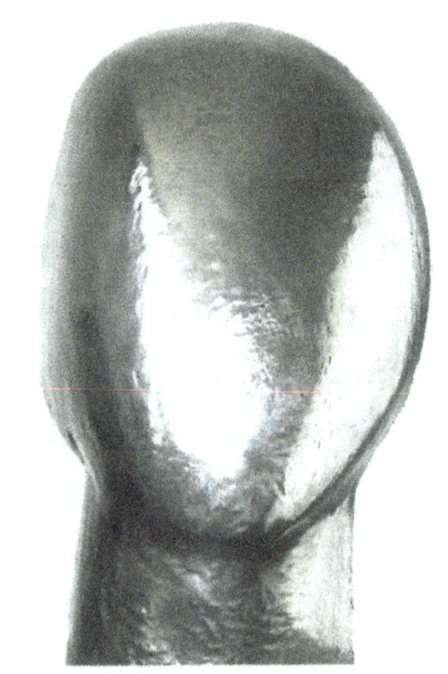

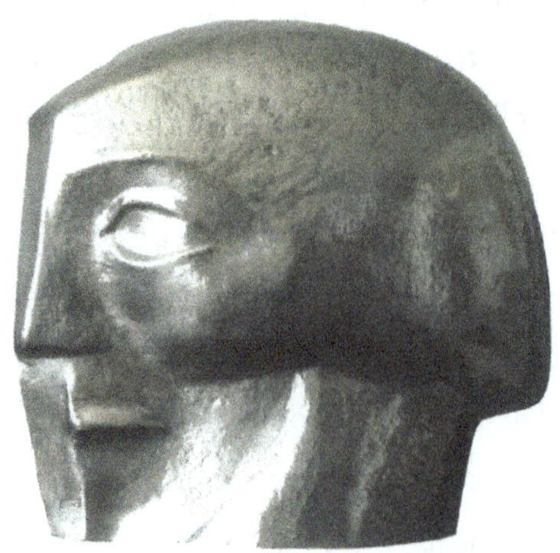

Plate 25

on the expression of the face in order to convey the meaning within the portrait. However, Cubism, at the beginning of the 20th century, completely reinvented the image of man's face. Instead of soft expressive portraits that sought to capture the essence of humanity through the face, Cubism, influenced by African masks with their distorted proportions, meant that the human face was no longer an indicator of identity. This radical change of artistic perception created a ripple effect that transformed not only modern art but also man's view of himself. Whilst totemic images from Africa (Benin) and Oceania (Easter Island) also played an important part in reshaping the artists' interpretation of the human face.

In *Les Demoiselles d'Avignon* (1907, Museum of Modern Art, New York), one of Picasso's best known paintings, he placed masks on at least two of the five figures within the portrait, a method he continued to use throughout his lifetime. Picasso spoke of this painting as his first 'exorcism painting'. The use of masks by artists reflects their desire to depict man as an entity isolated from other humans and from the rapidly changing world encircling him. These 'demons' from the modern world that haunted Picasso were exorcised from his soul and revealed to others through his use of masks. The human face which had possessed such great importance in the 19th century, represented for Picasso modern man's lack of identity and individuality. He saw the masks as a means of liberating humans from the oppression of sameness and dependence one on another.

The silver head created by Gross is of particular interest (Plate 25). Caroline Wagner observes that the size of the silver sheet out of which this head has been made would have been enough to make an archaic face mask, or the kind of helmet one could imagine on the heads of the heroes in Greek mythology or in the Trojan wars. Wagner comments: "But here there is no Pericles, no fighting, no mask. This object does not hide anything in its interior. It does not envelop any contents and make them invisible. It is not even the surface, the outer skin of anything. It is both form and content. There is no inside and no outside, or at least there is no interior that is not an exterior as well — and vice versa" (Wagner, 1991). The head then is neither mask nor sculpted bust and thus is a paradoxical object.

Masks are paradoxical because they enable a person to become what he is not; however, this disguise is complicated by the notion of the mask acting as an abstract symbol of duality. Only through recognising and accepting the transformation of a thing from one state to another is it possible to resolve the paradox, and without this ability or desire to reconcile a paradox, our acceptance of change is inconceivable.

One quality that this work possesses is playfulness — it is challenging, teasing and puzzling. This playfulness offers both illusions and allusions. One moment the head seems to be one thing, the next moment it is something else. An extraordinary feature of the head is that from the reverse side, the head takes on the appearance of a Cubist painting. The muted palette of bronze, pink, steel blue and grey is strongly reminiscent of certain portraits by Picasso. There can be few examples of a sculpture that mysteriously dissolves into what appears to be a painting.

The colours are a natural result of the process of oxidisation. With oxidisation we do not see the destruction of the metal, rather, the oxidisation forms a skin or patina on the metal that acts to protect the underlying surface and actually inhibits further chemical reaction. We know that some contemporary silversmiths deliberately seek to achieve an oxidised effect on their jewellery. After her husband's death Trude Sand insisted that the head should be kept highly polished and one must assume that this stricture applied solely to the exterior. What are the aesthetic consequences? Whilst the polished surface quite literally reflects back the external world, the oxidised interior invites the viewer into it. The untreated side provides an authentic face, whilst the polished side provides an artificial face.

The head is teasing insofar as it presents the viewer with a series of further paradoxes. Whilst the exterior of an object is usually that aspect that gains the viewer's attention, here it is the interior that appears to possess more character and meaning. What is particularly intriguing is that Gross is inviting us to see behind the mask, something that is rarely done. It is as if a taboo has been broken. To emphasise this feeling of gaining new insights, we are presented with a face in which the eye is dominant and rather like the Eye of Horus — the Ancient Egyptian symbol for indestructibility.

One of the most intriguing angles from which to view the head is from the back. Or is it the back? From one angle we seem to be presented with a human face stripped of all facial features. Gross would have been aware of the work of Constantin Brancusi, for he was working in Paris at the same time as Gross.

He would have known of Brancusi's minimalist representations of the human face — *The Sleeping Muse* (1910, Metropolitan Museum of Modern Art). The strongly ovate shape of the face of *The Sleeping Muse* intentionally suggests an egg — a symbol of birth or new life. In discussing the nature of his work Brancusi coined the striking aphorism that "simplicity is complexity resolved". So when one moves to a position to view the 'rear' of the head, the intrinsic complexity of the head magically resolves into a simple Brancusian ovoid.

So in this single artefact — the silver head — we have allusions not only to different artistic genres but also to symbols of considerable power — indestructibility, birth and rebirth. These, in turn, can be interpreted as signs of resurrection and hope — themes that Gross pursued throughout his life. But then the question will be asked: 'How can one be so confident that Gross was trying to communicate any of these messages?' The simple answer is that we cannot know. But that question rather misses the point. What Gross has succeeded in doing is stimulating the viewer to reflect on its meaning.

Let us now turn to the brass head shown in Plates 26. This bears a striking resemblance to the *moai*, the minimalistically styled monolithic statues found throughout Polynesia. The *moai* were carved in relatively flat planes with the faces bearing a haughty but enigmatic expression. The over-large heads have heavy brows, elongated noses with a distinctive fish hook shaped curl of the nostrils. The lips protrude in a thin pout. Like the nose, the ears are elongated and oblong in form. The jaw lines stand out against a truncated neck. While *moai* are often described simply as 'heads', they are, in fact, whole body statues. The function and use of the *moai* is still not known, although it is thought they were symbols of authority and power, both religious and political. To the people who erected and used them, they were repositories of sacred spirit. Carved stones in ancient Polynesian religions were believed to be charged by a magical spiritual essence.

Having lived in Paris, before, during and after the war, Gross would have been familiar with the main exhibits in The Louvre including an Easter Island *moai* (*Moai de l'île de Pâques*). The exhibit is similar in many respects to the head created by Gross. What probably appealed to Gross was how modern the human face depicted in the *moai* appeared. At first sight the head made by Gross seems

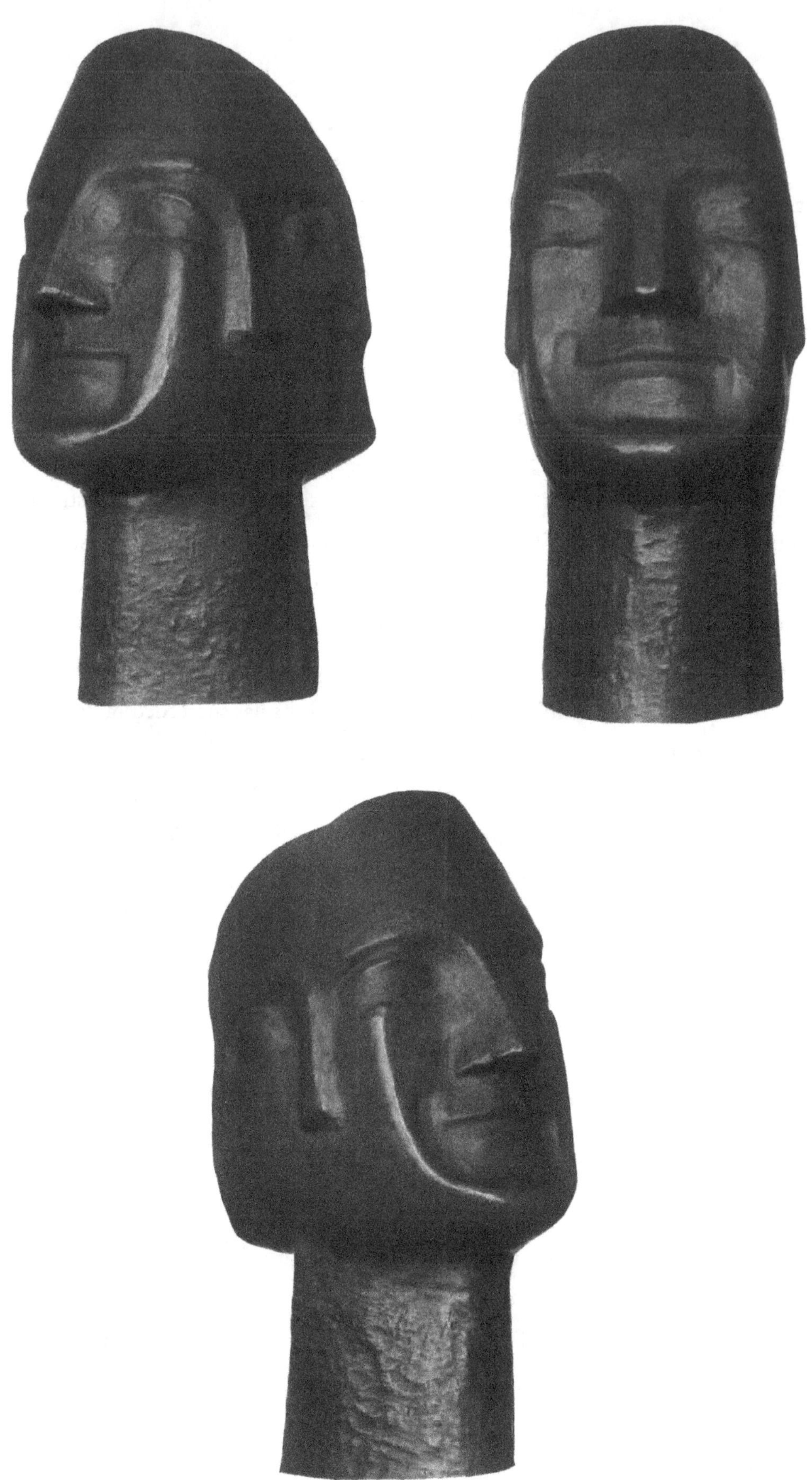

Plate 26

to possess the same solidity and monumentality as the *moai*, until one realises, on closer inspection, that it is a mask. It is hollow! This totemic head appears to bridge not only historical epochs but widely different civilisations. From a plain brass sheet and through the practised use of fire and hammer, a sculpture has been created which possesses a timeless resonance and meaning.

What is Gross seeking to say with the untitled mask shown in Plate 27? On the right, looking out from the mask, we have a conventional representation of a human face and on the left what appears to be a tribal facemask of some kind. Is Gross drawing a distinction here between our civilised and enlightened nature and our more primitive instincts and feelings which lie hidden? Some weight is lent to such an interpretation by the fact that the left side (sinister) is usually associated with malevolence, gloomy foreboding and evil, whilst the right side (dexter) is linked with benevolence, innocence and moral virtue. By presenting the head in the way he has, Gross may be indicating that humans are necessarily a mixture of both, although attempts to keep our weaknesses concealed meet with varying degrees of success.

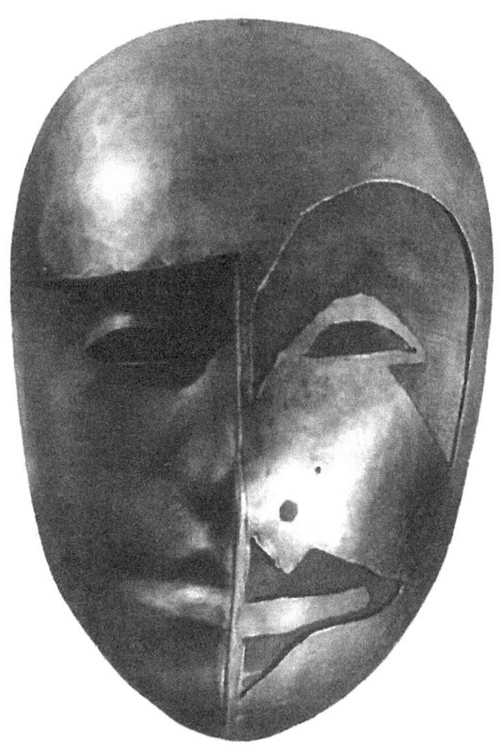

Plate 27

Gross' preoccupation with the theme of the mask was not confined to his sculpture, for it is very strongly in evidence in his paintings. Let us take the painting shown in Plate 28 which appears to show a carnival scene. An important feature in any carnival is the masquerade in which individuals hide their identity behind masks. However there is no attempt here at disguise either on the woman's part, as she is clearly shown unmasked, or on the bear's part as it clearly is a bear! Is Gross suggesting that it is only man who attempts to conceal his identity and that only by dispensing with the mask can man engage with joy and without inhibition in life's dance? Or are there some chauvinistic ideas here about how women and animals have no need of masks because they are more purely in tune with 'nature' and truth (Dimond, 2008)?

This painting illustrates one particular feature of Gross' work. Gross was a consummate craftsman yet many of his paintings convey the impression that they are sketches which are to be worked on later. It may be that he wanted to make the point that no painting can ever truly be finished for the task of the painter is to convey his immediate thoughts and feelings even if that means presenting something that is incomplete. The fact that at this time Gross' work was neither commissioned nor destined for sale may have played a part.

Another work (Plate 29) is difficult to interpret. One title that has been attributed to it is *'The legionnaire and the boy'*. Some caution should be exercised before accepting this title not just because Gross tended not to title his paintings but because it does not seem to tally with what one sees. There would appear to be four figures. There is the piper in the foreground facing to the right, the various parts of the pipes can be clearly seen. The second person who stands behind the piper appears to be a girl or woman, wearing a mantilla-like headdress, a collar of lace and a long white dress. The angle of her head suggests a demure demeanour or that she may be reading something in front of her. The third person who stands to the right is not easy to make out. Is he wearing a military kepi and cloak? Is this the legionnaire? The final person, if indeed it is a person, appears to be presiding over the occasion, whatever that occasion is. Or is the face actually a mask?

But does any of this really matter? Gross would no doubt be amused at this degree of speculation. What may have happened here and occurred in other paintings is that he started with a series of geometric shapes, played with them

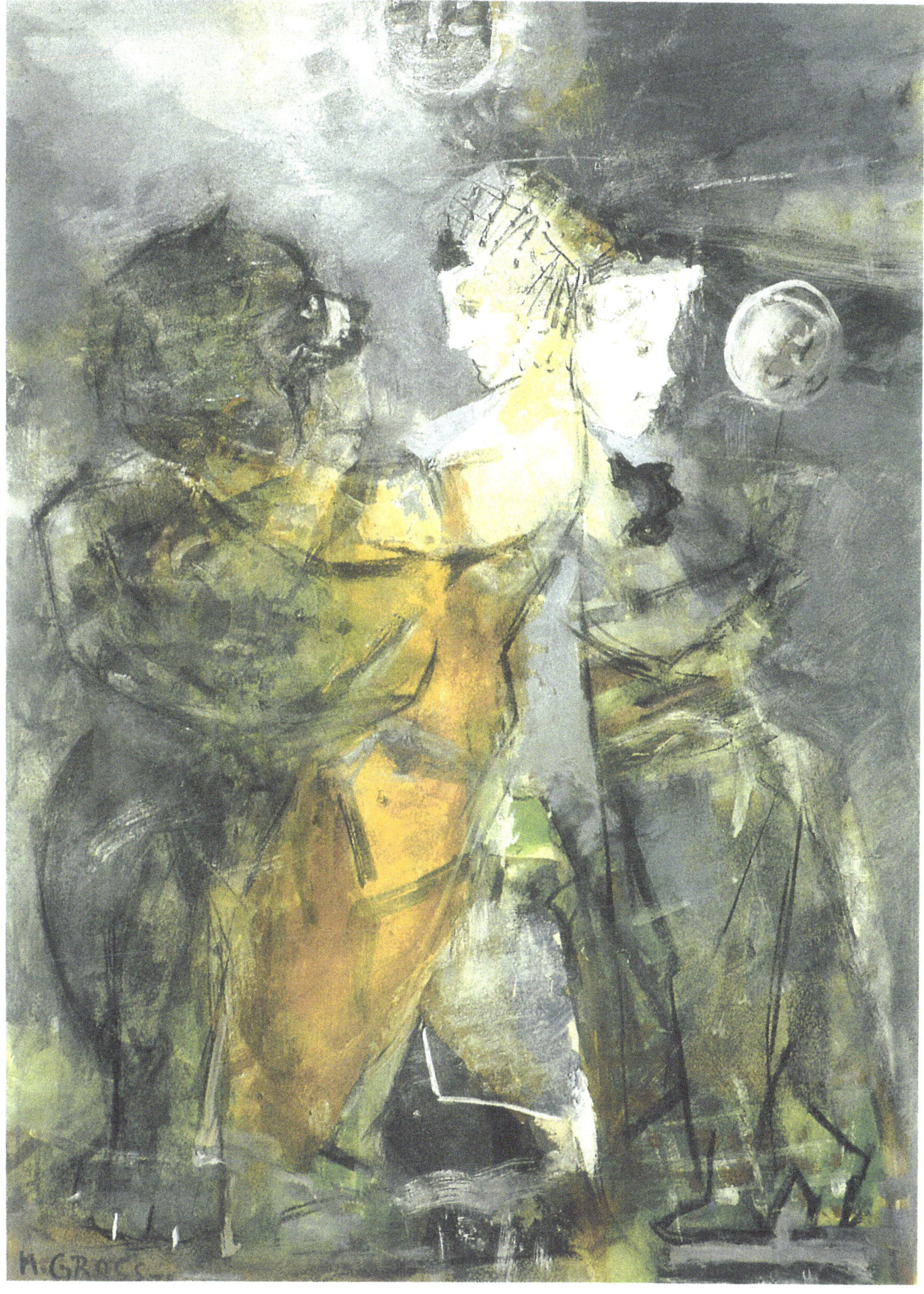

Plate 28

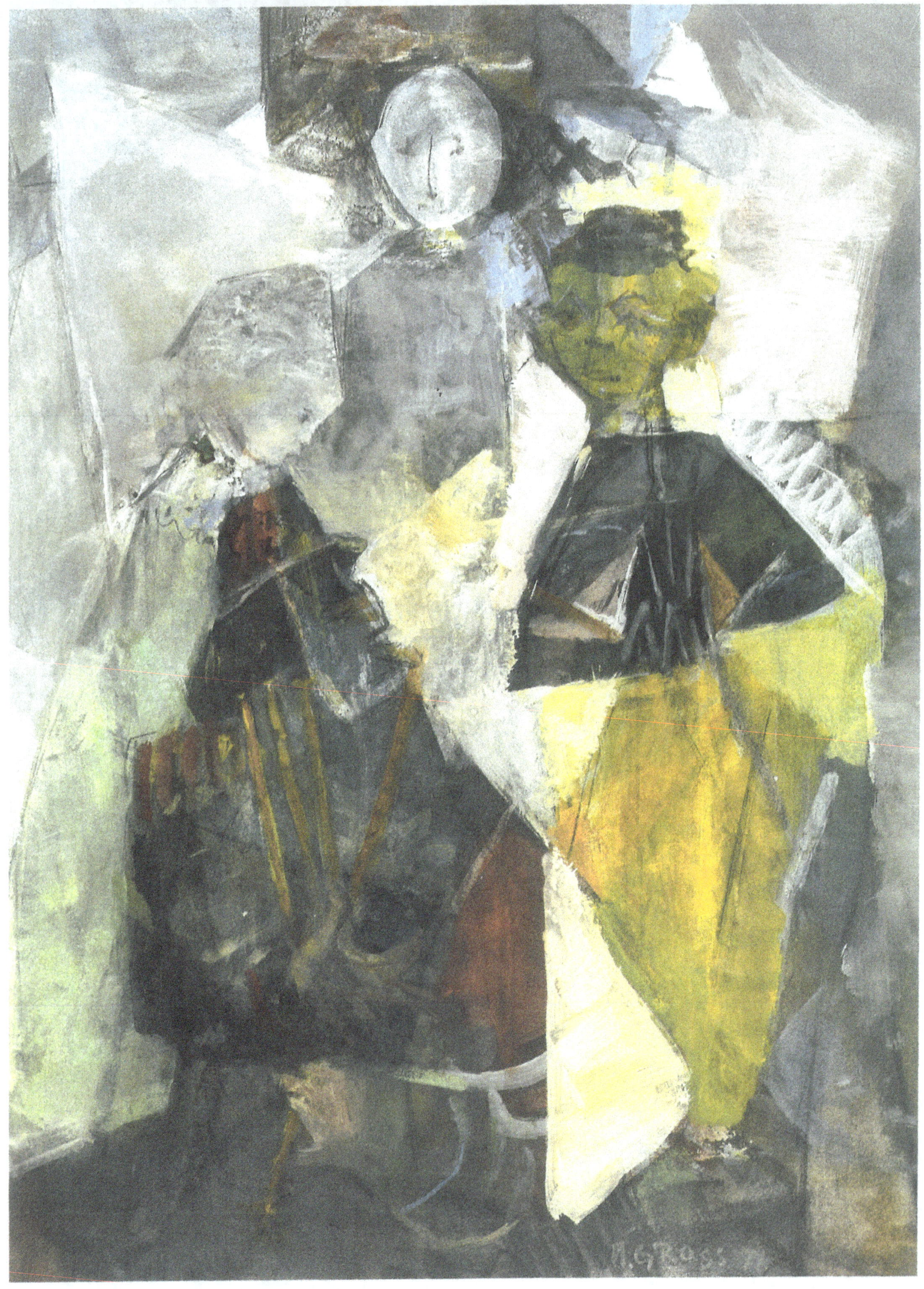

Plate 29

in different ways, and then gave to them human characteristics, where and when he was prompted to do so. In other words, Gross did not set out with the intent to depict a wedding scene with bride, groom and attendant piper, if that is what it is. It just happened that these figures began to emerge from the geometric patterns on the paper in front of him. It is also perfectly possible that Gross was teasing the viewer. As many of his paintings were hung in community rooms in the various Camphill estates, Gross may have simply wanted viewers to engage with the content. If it was a riddle without an answer, did that really matter if it had stimulated people to look at paintings?

Children and Camphill

Gross' work is unusual insofar as there are relatively few examples of children as principal subjects in either classical or modern art apart from the iconic representations of the Christ child, yet children feature strongly in his work. Not only does Gross take children as his main subjects, but he goes one step further and encourages the viewer to reflect upon the transient nature of childhood and all the vulnerabilities inherent in it. The challenge for the artist is to be able to convey that message without recourse to the cloyingly sentimental images that characterised much of Victorian illustrations depicting childhood. For the childhood portrayed at that time was in large measure a bogus one. Many of the children who appear closely and lovingly ensconced in the bosom of a devoted family were either in the care of a governess or attending a distant boarding school. There was also a tendency to represent children as innocent, angelic, appealing, attractive, obedient and gentle beings, whereas by nature they are, for at least some of the time, mischievous, naughty, unappealing, unattractive, wayward and wild. In some instances one rather suspects that the artist's patron would have preferred and valued a painting of his favourite dog or horse than a portrait of his family.

Gross does not present sentimental art that leads the viewer away from active engagement with the ambiguities and complexities of the real world. As Deborah Knight notes, sentimentality in art makes no demands upon us, requires no struggle, involves only a narrow range of feelings, arouses no thoughts or feelings about the real world: it represents a general failure of imagination (Knight, 1999). Gross, like König, was aware that the kind of social renewal they sought could only be achieved by creating a world that was more responsive to the needs of the child. This is social art, where the medium is being used to convey an ethical message, not simply about how one should care for and protect children but how societies, in general, should treat all vulnerable groups.

Where artists have taken children as legitimate subjects for paintings their work has tended to be criticised as sentimental. This was a judgement of some critics of the work of Joan Eardley who painted the children who lived in the decaying tenement districts of post-war Glasgow. Adult figures very rarely appeared in her work. Eardley's work may only have gained critical acceptance once it was realised that she was not a purveyor of kitsch. Eric Newton, the art critic of *The Guardian*, in a review of the last Joan Eardley exhibition in London in 1963 commented: "only in an occasional Goya do I remember the translation of small children into paint mixed so inseparably with warmhearted self-identification with the inner life of the child". Both Eardley and Gross succeeded in persuading the viewer to treat children as serious subjects by portraying them with compassion and without sentimentality.

When Gross was artist-in-residence in Aberdeen, a significant number of children attending the Camphill School were drawn from the districts in Glasgow with which Eardley would have been familiar. Thus there is a sense in which both Gross and Eardley were portraying children from similar backgrounds. Eardley's paintings demonstrate that, notwithstanding personal circumstance, the child possesses an inner resilience that transcends that circumstance, however disadvantageous. Eardley was particularly attracted by the friendliness and community spirit in these districts. Both Eardley and Gross were commenting in different ways upon the importance of a sense of community. By the time of Eardley's death in 1963 many of these old tenement districts had been levelled to the ground and residents transferred to soulless high-rise estates on the periphery of the city. In the process that strong sense of community that had so appealed to Eardley had been destroyed.

One might argue that Eardley and Gross differ in that Eardley tended to focus almost exclusively on the child, whereas Gross almost always sets the child in the context of a relationship with one or more adults. Whilst Eardley stressed the independent identity of the child, Gross highlighted the importance of interdependence — an essential feature of life in a Camphill community. The life-sharing aspect of Camphill community life is one of its defining features, as this ensures that the principles of dignity and mutual respect can be meaningfully translated into practice. And it is this mutual relationship that provides the cohesive force that binds together the different elements of a community: it is the mortar without which the communal edifice would collapse.

Japanese Noh

Gross' paintings which involve children do not lend themselves to easy interpretation. In Plate 30 we have a picture of a young woman playing a harp and behind her looking out of the picture we have a Japanese Noh player. Is Gross intimating that Western artistic traditions are impoverished, if they 'turn their back' on Eastern traditions? The Noh player looking out of the picture suggests that a direct approach is being made to the viewer.

Noh is a classical Japanese performance which combines elements of dance, drama, music and poetry into one highly aesthetic stage art. It has been enacted in Japan since the 14th century. By tradition, Noh actors and musicians, who are almost always male, never rehearse for performances together. Instead, each actor, musician and choral chanter practises his basic movements, songs and dances independently or under the tutelage of a senior member of the school. Thus, the tempo of a given performance is not set by a single performer or director but established by the interaction of all the performers together. In general, Noh plays are not very dramatic, although they are beautiful, since the text is full of poetical allusions and the dances, though slow, are extremely elegant. It is this very beauty, which makes Noh a living art form. Noh also antedates many developments in contemporary theatre, such as absence of scenery or minimalist stage-sets and the symbolic use of props.

The musicians and choirs in Noh plays typically wear a formal *montsuki* kimono (black and adorned with five family crests), whilst the most commonly used prop is the fan which is carried by all performers regardless of role. The

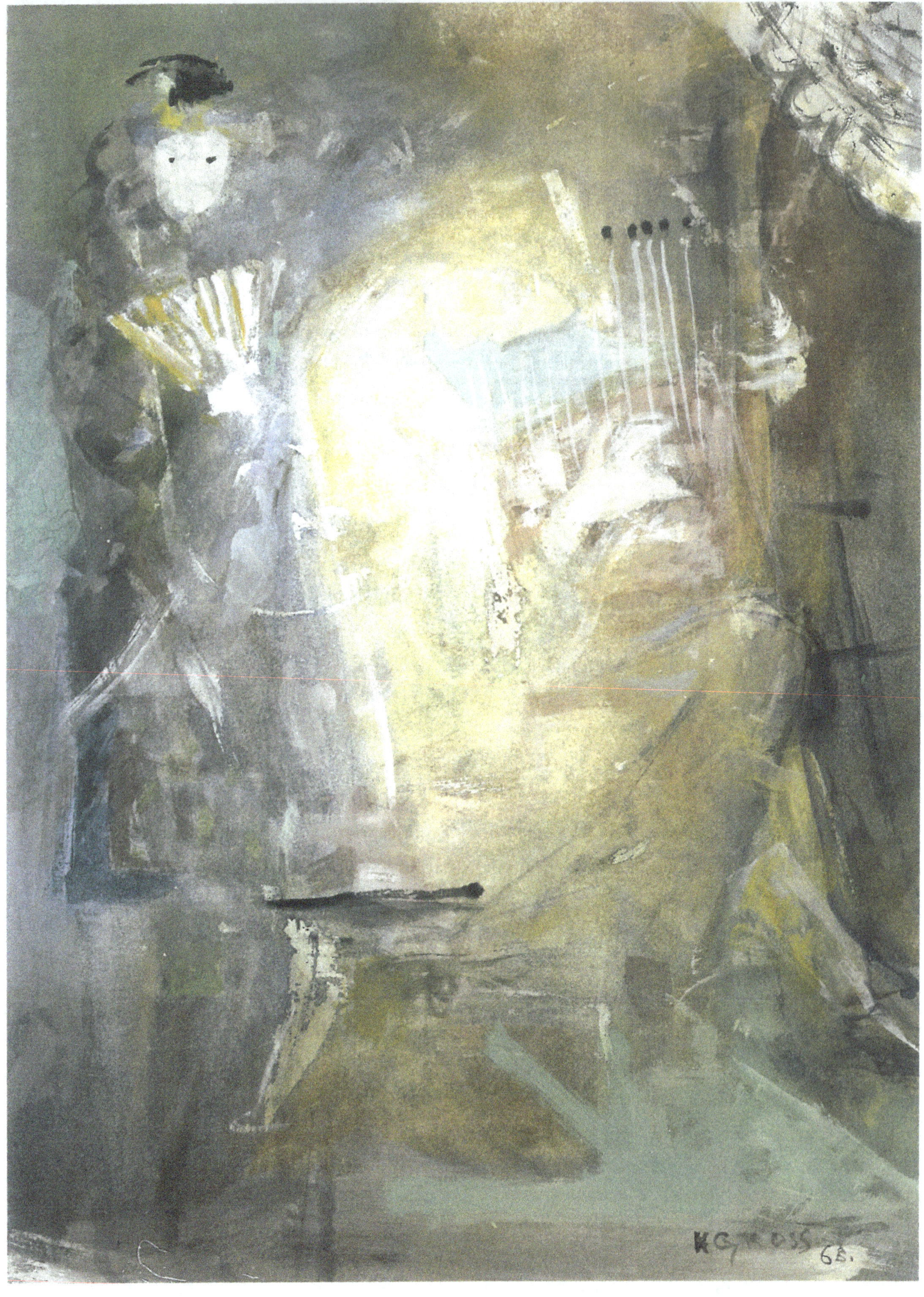

Plate 30

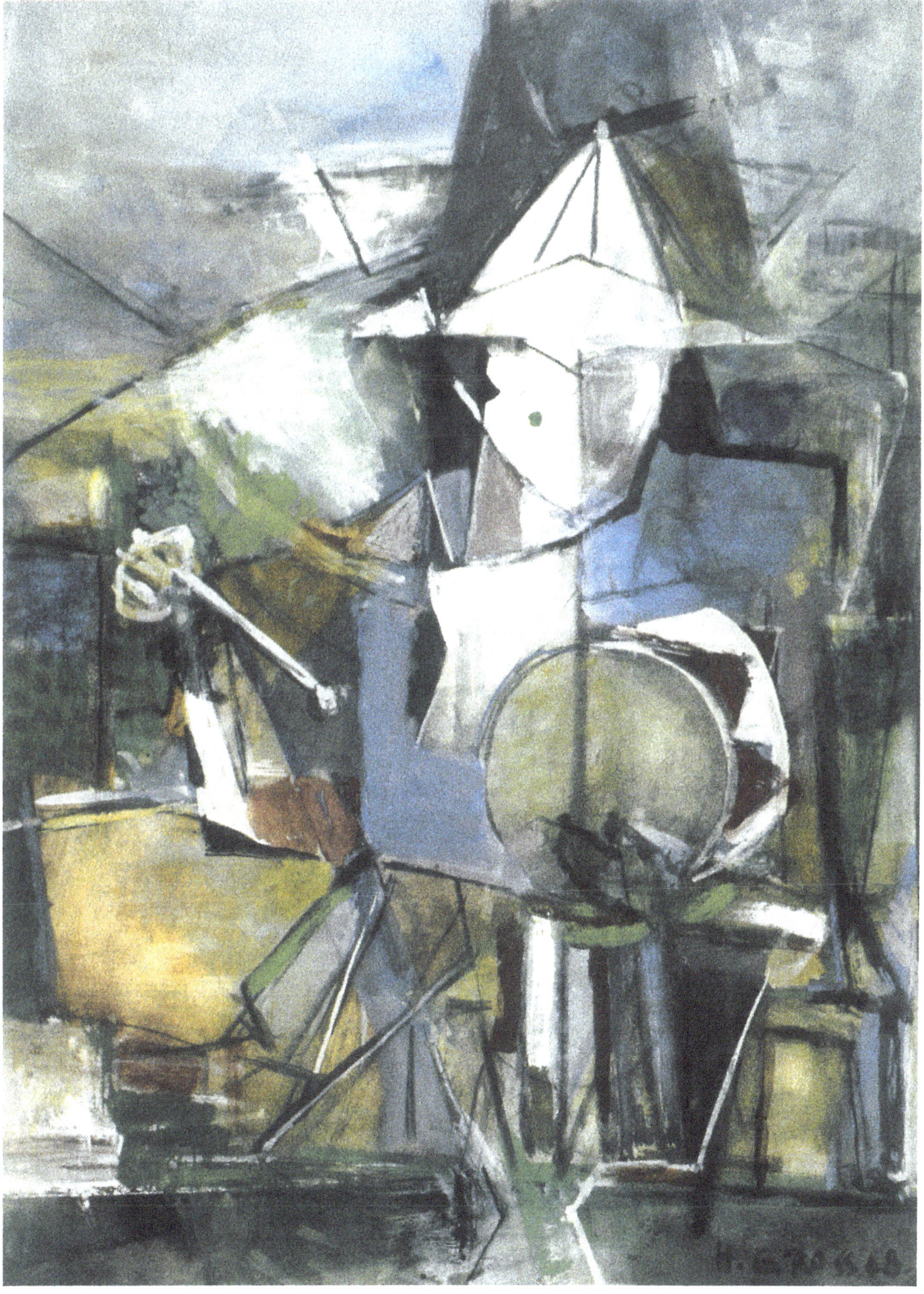

Plate 31

masks worn by Noh players are carved from wood, often cedar, which is then gessoed and painted. Some of the most moving works of sculptural art in Japan are Noh masks.

What is the relevance of this picture to those working in Camphill? It would appear that the harpist is performing by herself seemingly oblivious to her surroundings. Noh players, on the other hand, are engaged in a collective performance in which their individuality is subsumed within that of the group. Is this a commentary on the cult of the individual in Western society with its attendant self-centredness which those in Camphill should reject?

Plate 31 tells us something about another feature of Camphill life. In attempting to communicate effectively with a child, the carer has to fall into step with the child, so that they 'dance to the same tune.' It is necessary, therefore, to listen to the 'beat' that the child provides. The child and the carer then search for ways to establish and maintain that joint rhythm, in a mutually inclusive way. It is necessary to learn to listen, to look, and explore in a new way, the pulse of groups with whom one works. Rhythm is crucially important for it provides an impulse and framework that enables often bewildered and disoriented children to experience for the first time a measure of stability, security and predictability. Rhythm is the living pulse that sustains the work of a community (Maier, 2004). But as Maier has pointed out the binding qualities of rhythm must not be confused with the lockstep quality of the single drummer's efforts to gain conformity. True rhythmicity, in contrast, requires a process of mutual engagement and inclusion, a response to the beat of several drummers.

Kaspar Hauser

In Plate 32 we have a young child sitting on a rocking horse who is accompanied by a person with a blackened face or mask. Is this an allusion to Kaspar Hauser — a figure of mystery whose life is celebrated in Camphill communities? Kaspar was a child who lived in a tiny cave somewhere in the German countryside without any human contact except for a mysterious masked man who appeared from time to time to give him food. His only company was a rocking horse. One day in 1828 the masked man appeared and took Kaspar to the middle of Nuremberg

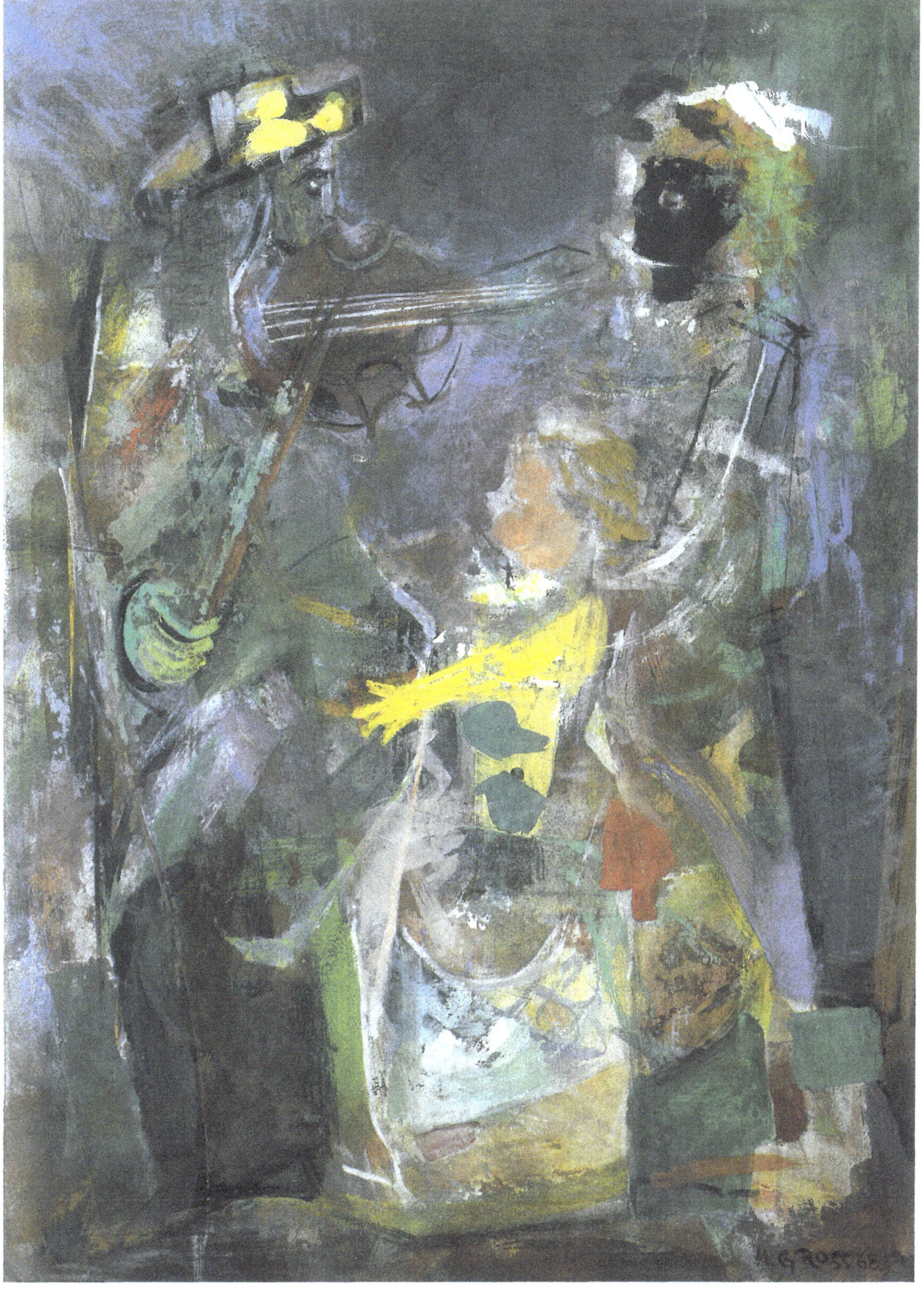

Plate 32

and left him there holding a letter of introduction asking for him to be inducted into a certain cavalry regiment. Kaspar, who eventually learned to speak, read and write in a rudimentary way had an obsession in asking people simple questions that they could not answer and which made them feel uncomfortable. A major difficulty for Kaspar was that he could not understand the basic dynamics of human relationships thus ending up in a state of social limbo. In order to survive he was totally reliant on the charity of others. In 1829 he claimed that a man with a blackened face assaulted him and then in 1833 he was killed by a masked stranger in Ansbach.

Kaspar possessed many of the characteristics of the autistic spectrum, in particular his inability to decode the social rules that govern interpersonal conduct. Yet that difficulty has a value because it means that social behaviour that we take for granted as normal is challenged. The autistic child has an innocence not possessed by others and it is this innocence that makes non-autistic people uncomfortable. It is believed that Kaspar came from a noble family in Baden which wanted to distance itself from the stigma of being known to have a handicapped family member. The role of the fiddler in this painting is not clear. Given that this painting is intended for staff in Camphill, Gross may be suggesting that one effective way of communicating with autistic children is through music. There is within the structure and rhythmic patterns of music a language to which many autistic children can relate. Another way of interpreting this painting is that, if staff exercise their imagination and undertake a conscientious search, they will find some way of communicating. In the 1960s, when this picture was painted, this would have been a revolutionary idea.

We are presented in Plate 33 with a figure cradling a baby in his left arm and holding a mask in his right hand. A curious feature is that rather than a conventional facemask, this is the kind of all-enclosing hollow iron mask worn by prisoners in centuries past. The red, yellow and black diamond pattern of the costume, when coupled with the cross-gartered red hose, seems to point to the figure being Harlequin; yet the whitened face, the conical white hat and the gloved hands suggest Pierrot! So who is actually portrayed here? What is the significance of this ambiguity and ambivalence? When we think of Harlequin and Pierrot, we tend to associate certain distinctive characteristics with each one. Is

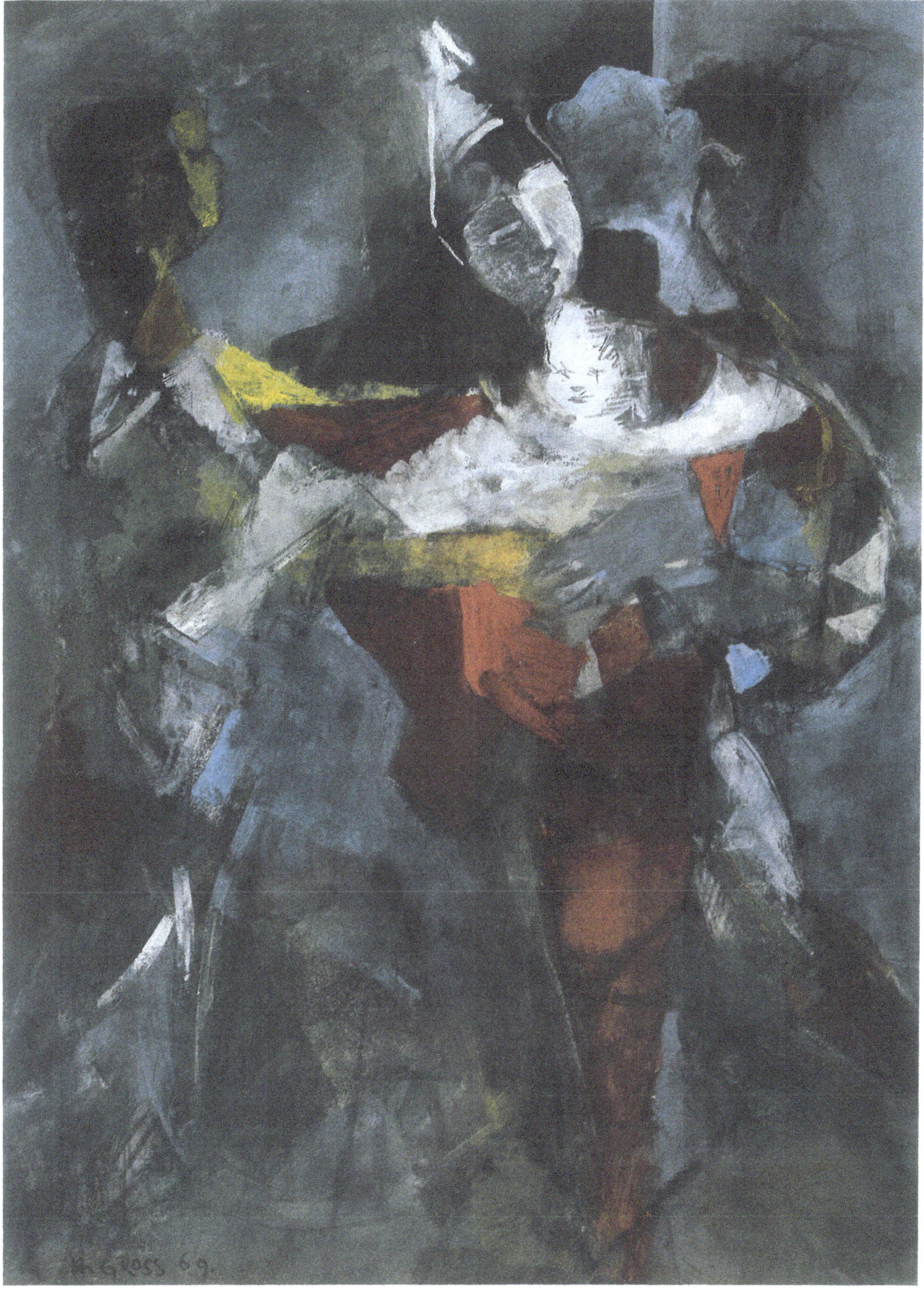

Plate 33

Gross encouraging the viewer not to prejudge people by their outward appearance? In other words, the more closely we look the more likely it is that we will find in people unexpected facets.

Strong primary colours coupled with the free and expressive manner in which the paint has been applied make a strong and disconcerting visual impact. It is unsettling not simply because of the subject matter but because of the way in which the composition has been structured. The arrangement of the legs of the central figure indicates that he is in a state of disequilibrium.

Particularly disquieting is the apparent threat that the mask which is held by the central figure may be placed over the child's head. The sight of a potentially suffocating mask approaching the head of an innocent and vulnerable child is disturbing. Gross may be alluding to the fact that children, if they are to cope with all that life has to throw at them, need the time and freedom to develop a clear sense of who they are. Pupil records showed that a significant number of children attending the School in the 1960s came from backgrounds characterised by acute psychological and social deprivation in which they had failed to develop a clear sense of identity. Thus the carers had the responsibility of looking after and responding to children who were not simply bewildered and angry at the world at large but also suspicious and frightened of adults. The message for carers is the need to offer the child constancy of affection, consistency in approach and unwavering commitment notwithstanding their outward 'appearance'.

The dominant feature in Plate 34 is the eye of the child looking out at and inviting the viewer into the picture. The subdued tones of the palette used in this painting convey an impression of a tender and caring relationship between the child and the two adults — possibly nurses — who stand on either side of him. There is no mawkish sentimentality in this relationship. The painting successfully encapsulates the essence of Camphill philosophy and practice, where the child is placed at the centre of its work. It is interesting to set Gross' painting alongside the bronze sculpture — *The Great Mother* — created by his teacher Waldemar Raemisch (Plate 10). Both highlight, but in quite different ways, the importance of the care, comfort and guidance that adults can offer children. The stiff and passive monumentality of the bronze sculptures in Philadelphia fail to capture the essence of a caring relationship. However, Gross' experience of living

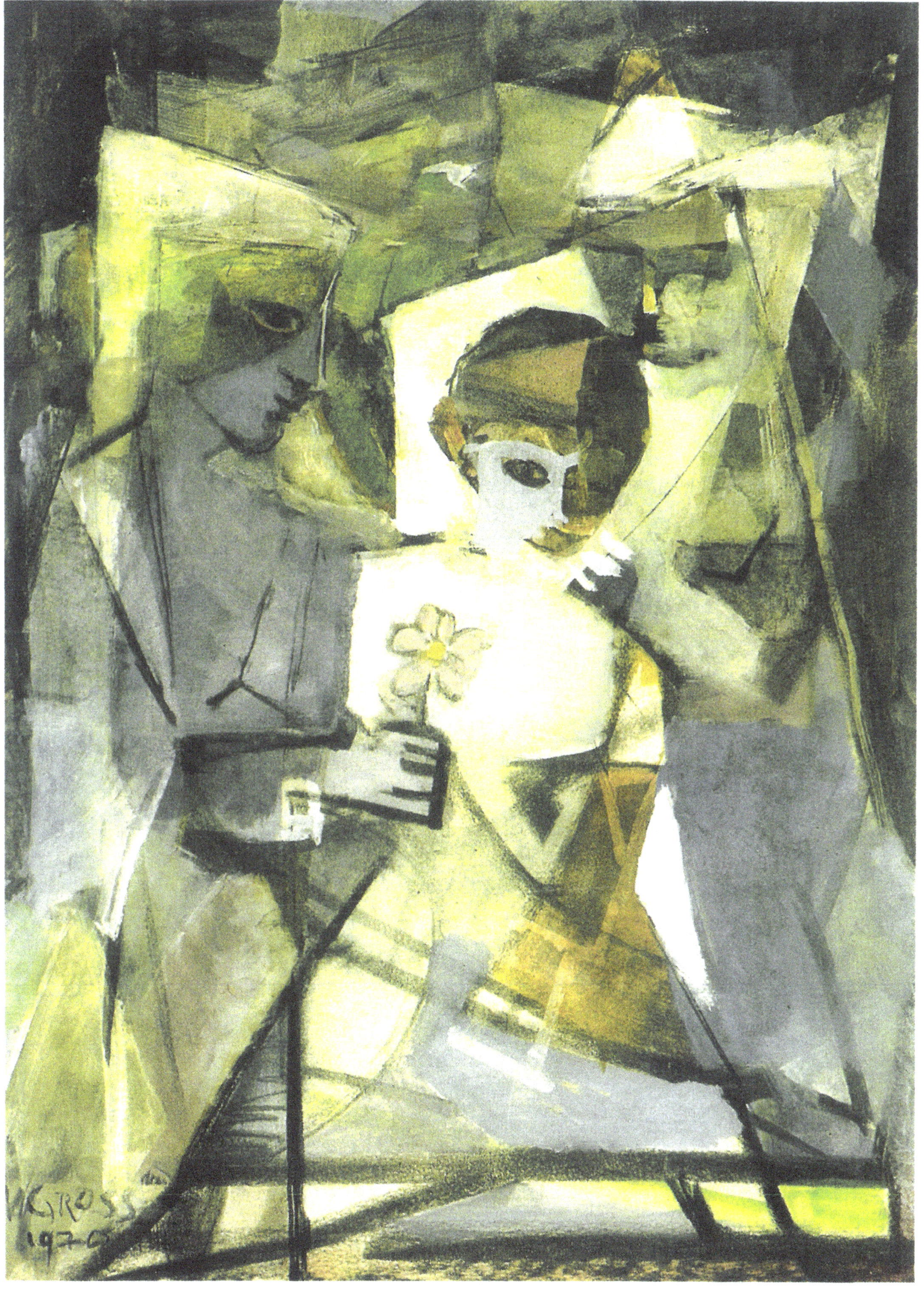

Plate 34

in a community dedicated to the care of vulnerable children and young people enabled him to communicate in a direct way the tender and supportive character of the adult-child relationship.

In Plate 35, which shows two children playing, Gross may be wishing to remind adult viewers in the school community of the importance of play in a child's life. It is not an incidental and trivial activity engaged in by a child but an important part of a child's physical, social and moral development. Play is the natural way for children to make sense of, and internalise, a whole range of experiences. It offers the opportunity to explore ways of being, of establishing identity and building self-esteem. The way in which the children's bodies intersect geometrically may be intended to convey the importance of social interaction, while the rings give an impression of vigorous movement. The smile on the face of the child wearing the tartan bonnet is perhaps a reminder that play is intended as an enjoyable experience. The content of this painting has a strong contemporary relevance. Play, whether formalised within the context of games, or recreational activities, or stemming from the creative imagination of the individual child appears to have no place in the present day mainstream curriculum. The consequence is educational, cultural and social impoverishment. But as Gross recognised an individual's spiritual development is dependent upon opportunities for free and creative self-expression.

In Plate 36 we have the juxtaposition of the angular mask-like face of the woman with the more realistically portrayed face of the child. What is Gross seeking to communicate to the viewer? Is he suggesting that in the presence of children adults tend to conceal their identity behind a mask dictated by the pressure of social conventions? The child appears to be slightly behind the woman and looking questioningly at her. Children often find the behaviour of adults difficult to comprehend. Essentially, this painting was intended to be seen by adults in a residential childcare setting. Is Gross intimating that the care offered by the adult has to be genuine and unconditional and not feigned — not least because most children are sophisticated enough to make that distinction? Whilst adults may attempt to hide behind a mask, children can frequently see through it.

Intriguingly the painting in Plate 37 departs from Gross' customary semi-abstract form. The subject may at first sight appear somewhat bizarre until one

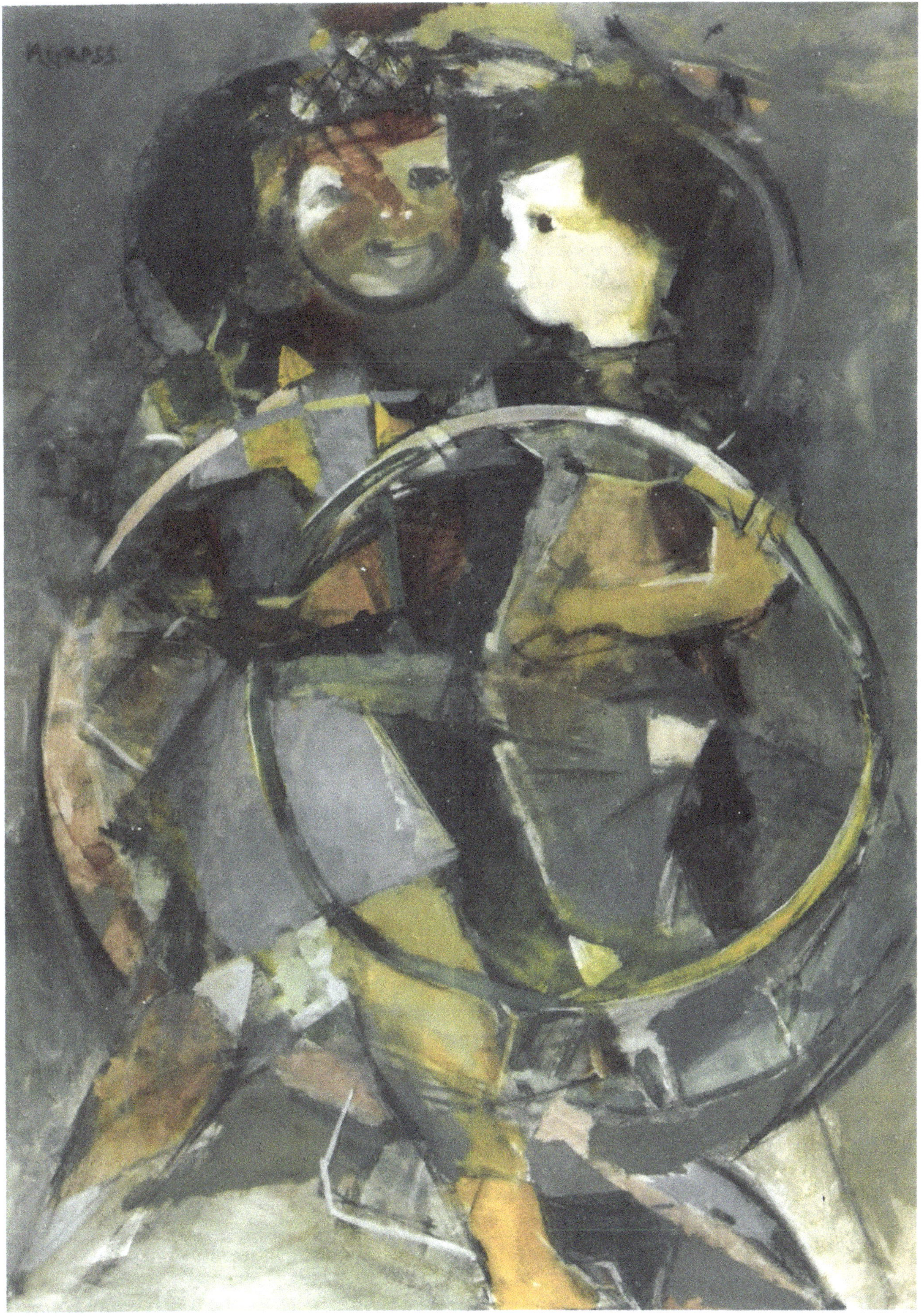

Plate 35

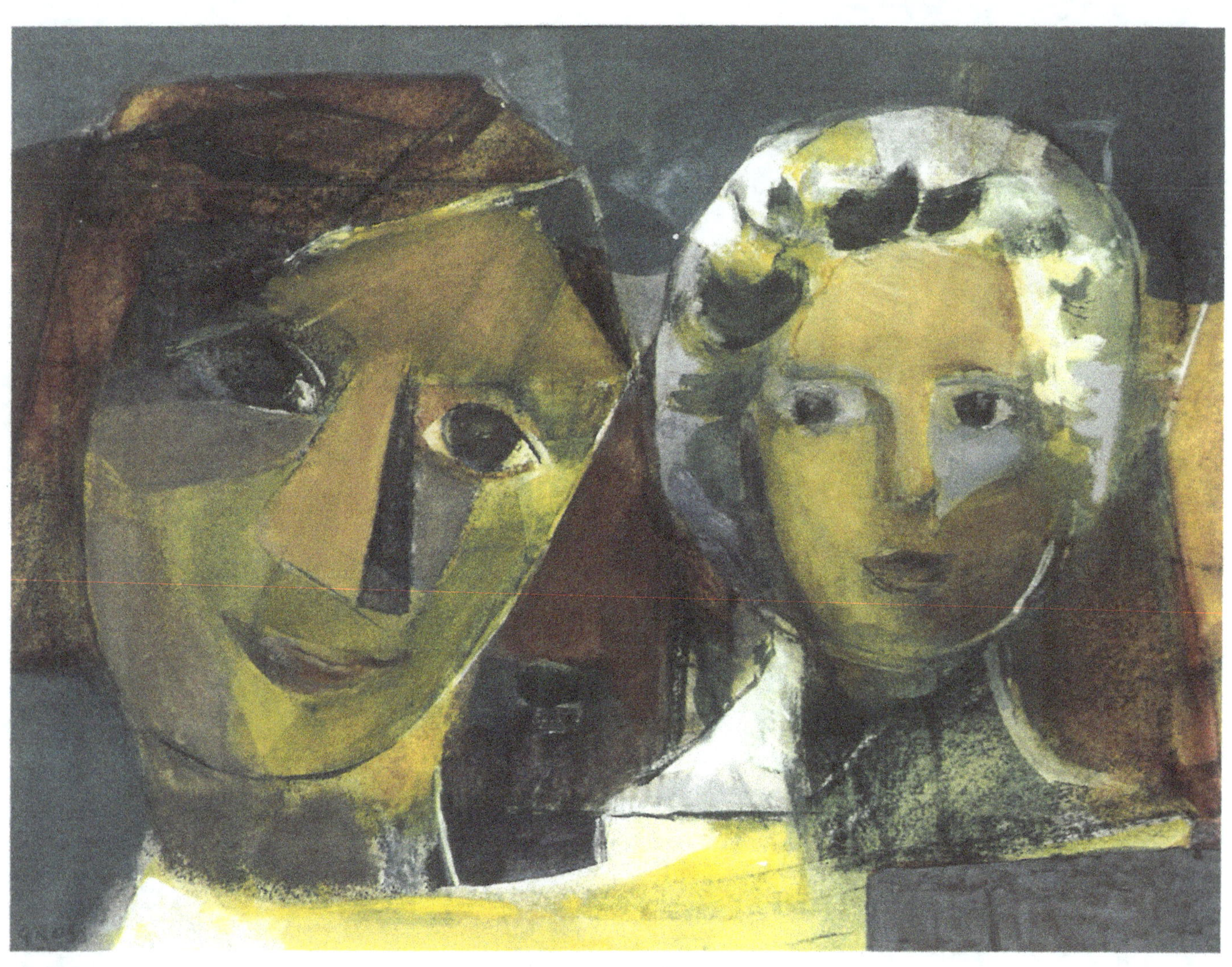

Plate 36

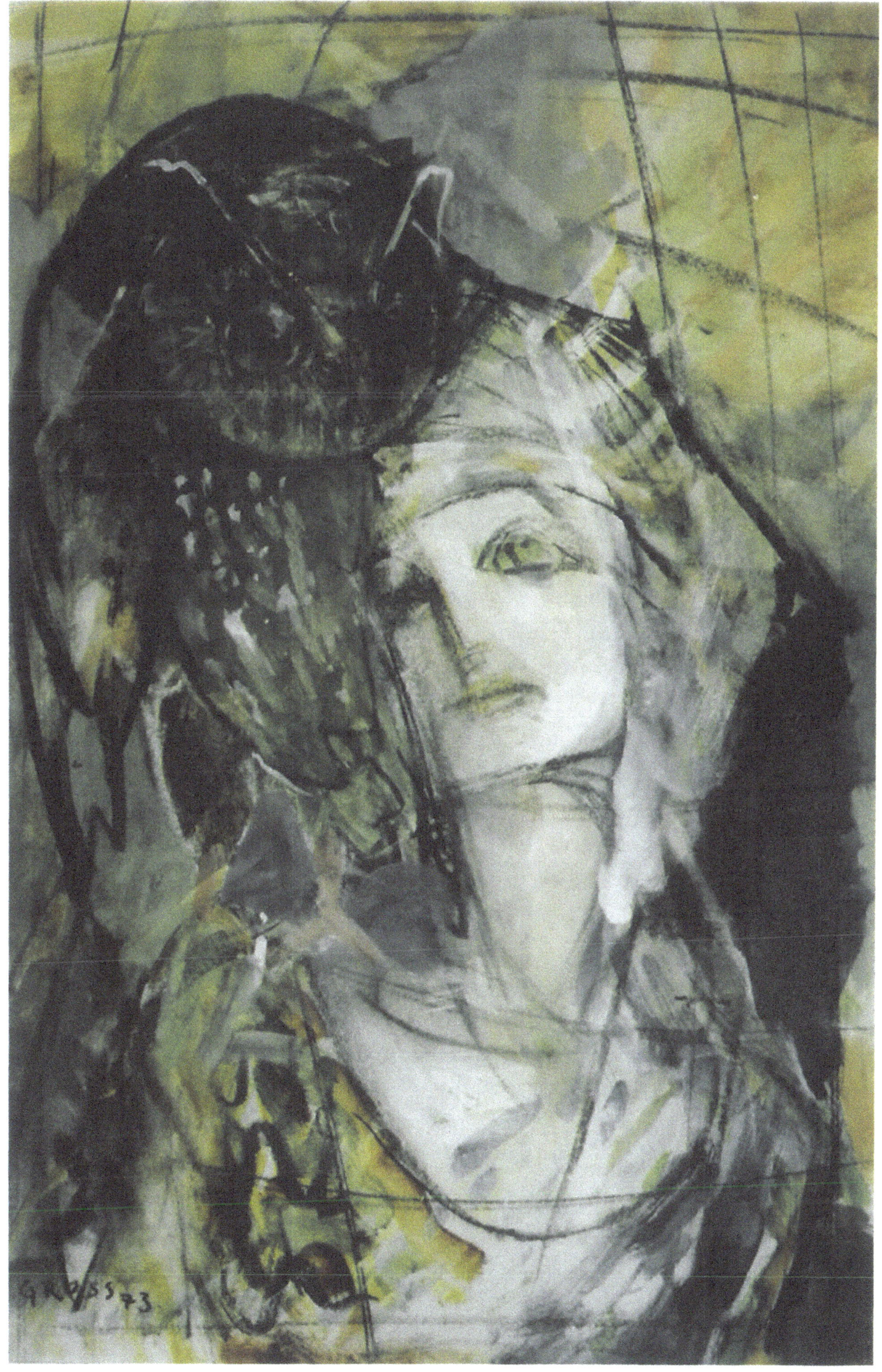

Plate 37

realises that the woman in the painting is Athena — the goddess of wisdom. Athena is frequently depicted with an owl either on her head or shoulders. As for the owl itself, in Western culture it has two major symbolic meanings, one is as an incarnation of wisdom and the other a harbinger of death or evil. There is something in the pose of the owl that suggests menace. As Gross never explained the meaning of his paintings it is necessary to be cautious in attempting an explanation. Could it be that only in death do we achieve true wisdom — a possible allusion to anthroposophical beliefs? Or could it be that only through engaging in the arts and crafts — painting, sculpting, weaving, pottery, wood and metal work — does one gain a true appreciation of and respect for our material and spiritual existence, for Athena was also the patroness of arts and crafts — activities strongly promoted in Camphill communities. But could this be a barbed message directed at those within Camphill communities who questioned the value and purpose of arts and crafts in the life of the community? Or was this more broadly an attack on those who saw no place for artistic creativity at all?

In Plate 38 we have a reflection of a face in a mirror. The ruff at the neck suggests a favourite subject for a number of Post-Impressionists painters. Is this Pierrot looking into the mirror and out at the viewer? The viewer therefore sees not the face of Pierrot but his reflection. In this instance no mask is required to conceal identity. As with Édouard Manet's *The Bar at the Folies-Bergère* (1882, Courtauld Institute of Art Gallery, London), mirrors can be employed to explore the idea that appearances can be deceptive and pose the question of whether we can ever see things as they really are.

Camphill Hall

One of the reasons that Karl König invited Gross to Aberdeen was to create a number of sculptures for the newly constructed Camphill Hall that was to be the spiritual heart of the Camphill Movement. Plate 18 shows Michael the Archangel representing peace and harmony, whilst Plate 19 shows Raphael the Archangel for healing. Their significance reflects König's endeavour to develop at Camphill the discipline of curative education or as it is still known in Germany — *Heilpädagogik* — literally healing pedagogy. What the photographs of these

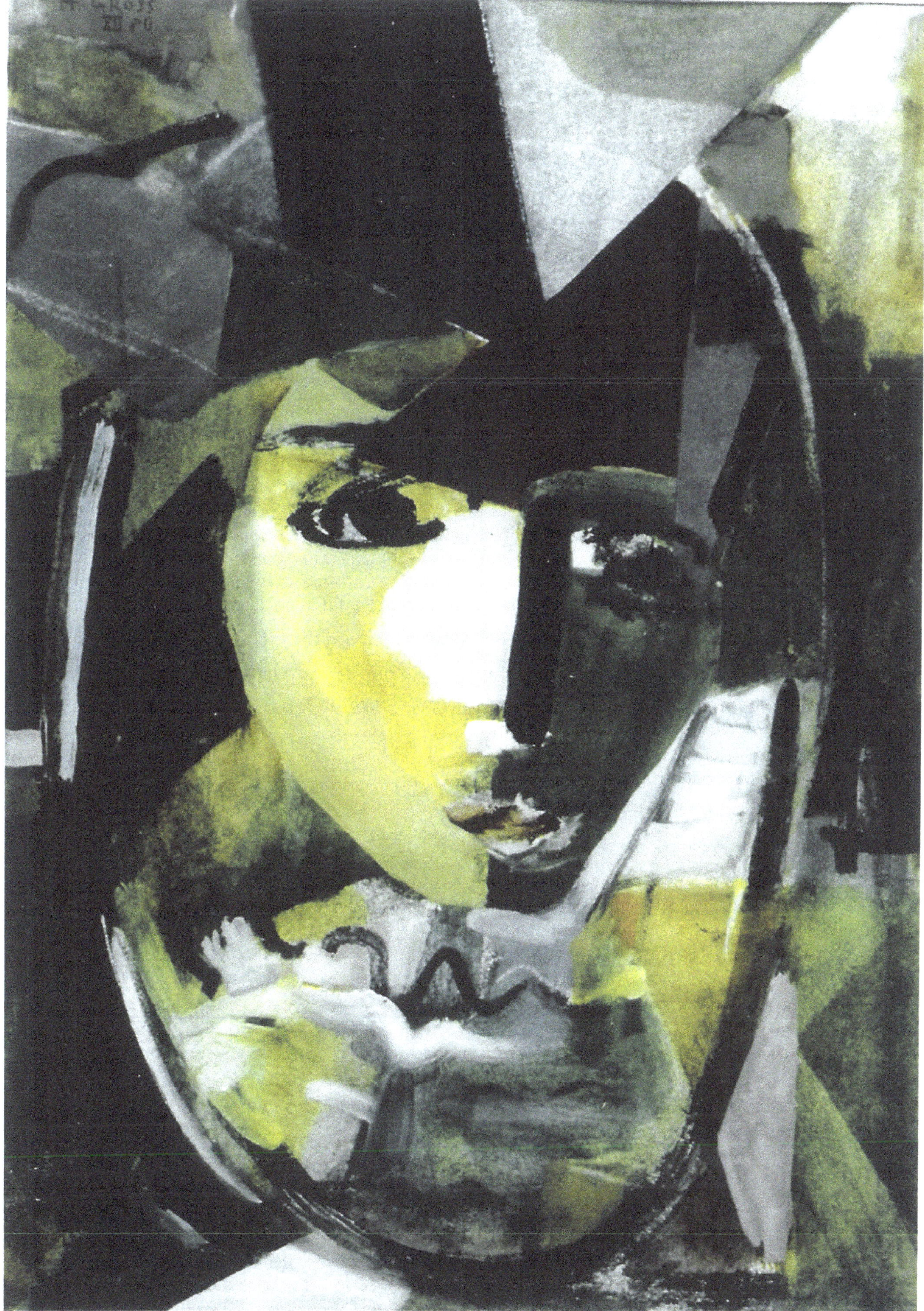

Plate 38

statues fail to convey is their size, for both are over two metres in height. Their location in the Hall is high on opposing walls.

Through long laborious physical effort Gross hammered featureless sheets of aluminium into three powerful and poetic images. The process of creating these statues brought Gross close to total despair. On at least one occasion he hurled his hammer at the sheet in a fit of exasperation. The viewer may not appreciate the very high degree of technical difficulty involved in creating these statues. The task for Gross was particularly difficult, as he had to stand behind the metal sheet he was hammering into shape. Gross obviously needed an intimate knowledge of the qualities of the material he was working with, a clear visual memory of what he had done as he could not see it, and an understanding of what he had to do on the 'reverse' face in order to achieve the subtle effects he desired. The statues constitute a technical tour de force.

The sculpture shown in Plate 20 is of quite a different character and depicts someone in prayer or meditation. Gross has refined the idea of prayer down to its absolute essence. The block upon which the left elbow rests projects from the sculpture and conveys an impression of great strength and solidity. Gross may also have wanted to indicate that the purpose of prayer rests on a firm biblical foundation and that through prayer man is given strength. Here is none of the gloomy introspection which so characterised his other religious work.

We know that in the mid-1960s when considering the design of and method of creating the stained glass windows for Camphill Hall, Gross had visited Pluscarden Abbey, a Benedictine community in Morayshire, founded as an Abbey by King Alexander II of Scotland in 1230. The Abbey experienced a very chequered history for it was burnt down in 1390 probably by the Wolf of Badenoch and from that point went into an irreversible decline so that by the beginning of the 19th century the Abbey was in ruins. However in 1948 a Benedictine community was re-established at Pluscarden and ambitious plans for the restoration of the buildings put in place. In 1974 it was once more re-instated as an Abbey.

As virtually all of the Pluscarden's stained glass had been lost it was necessary to create new windows. Whilst the main technique employed at Pluscarden was coloured glass cut to shape and joined by lead strips, a new technique was introduced which involved cutting and faceting thick slabs of glass known as *dalles de verre* (literally glass paving slabs) and setting them in a matrix of either epoxy resin or concrete. An appealing feature of the *dalles de verre* windows at Pluscarden recognised by the monks is the way in which the windows sparkle like jewels when in direct sunlight.

The person responsible for this innovation was Sadie McLellan (1914–2007) who was one of the foremost stained glass artists in Scotland. In 1959 she had completed her first experimental window in this new medium which was subsequently installed in Alloa Parish Church in 1960. She was then invited to Pluscarden Abbey and was responsible for the round window (oculus) in the North Wall of the North Transept of the Abbey which depicts the Woman of Revelation and The Great Red Dragon. Nothing of this size in stained glass had been attempted before in Scotland and it took three years to complete (1964–1967). To many people the work of McLellan represented the high water mark of 20th century stained glass in Scotland. Because of her fearless and trenchant independence of thought and action in all she did, she particularly endeared herself to the poet Hugh Macdiarmid who saw in her a kindred spirit. His poem *The Terrible Crystal* was dedicated to her.

Whilst Gross was responsible for the design of the windows in Camphill Hall, he was helped in their construction by his pupil Volker Gebhard. Recollecting the construction phase Gebhard acknowledged that both were novices at working with stained glass. The technique, in which the glass pieces were set in epoxy resin on a base sheet, was a relatively new and untried one. It was chosen because it offered the fullest flexibility in meeting the needs of the design. Progress was slow as Gross needed to consider carefully the location of each piece of glass. Nothing was decided until he was confident that it would add to the impact of the 'life fork' motif: one representing the past and the other the future. It took two years to bring the project to completion (Gebhard, 1988). (Plates 39–41)

The dominant feature in both stained glass windows is the Y figure. What is its significance? Throughout late antiquity, the Y was an accepted symbol of pagan ethics, of the choice between the hard path of virtue (right) and the easy path of vice (left). The Y can also be seen as a tree symbol related to the Christian cross and the Greek letter T (tau). Paintings in 15th Century Northern Europe

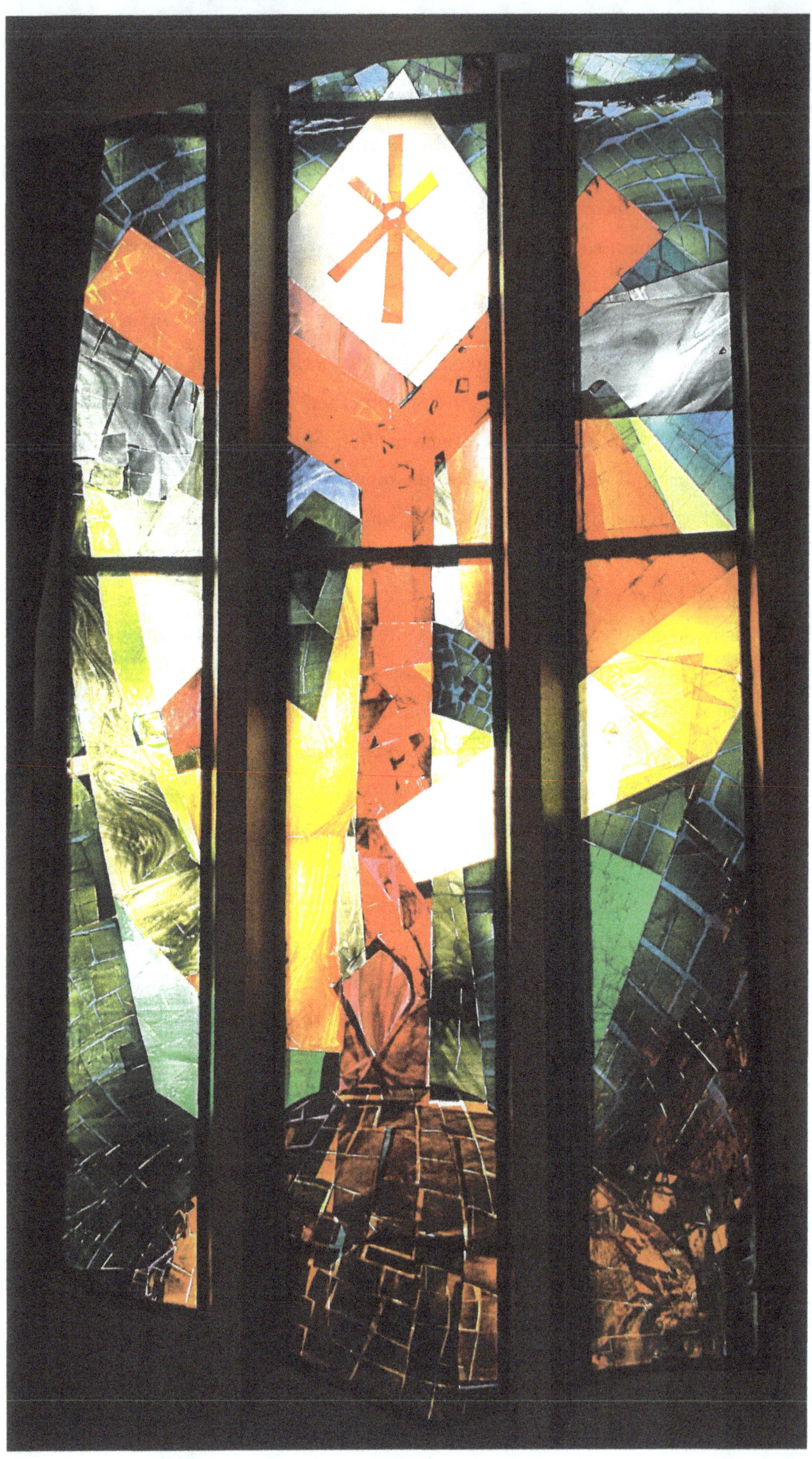

Plate 39

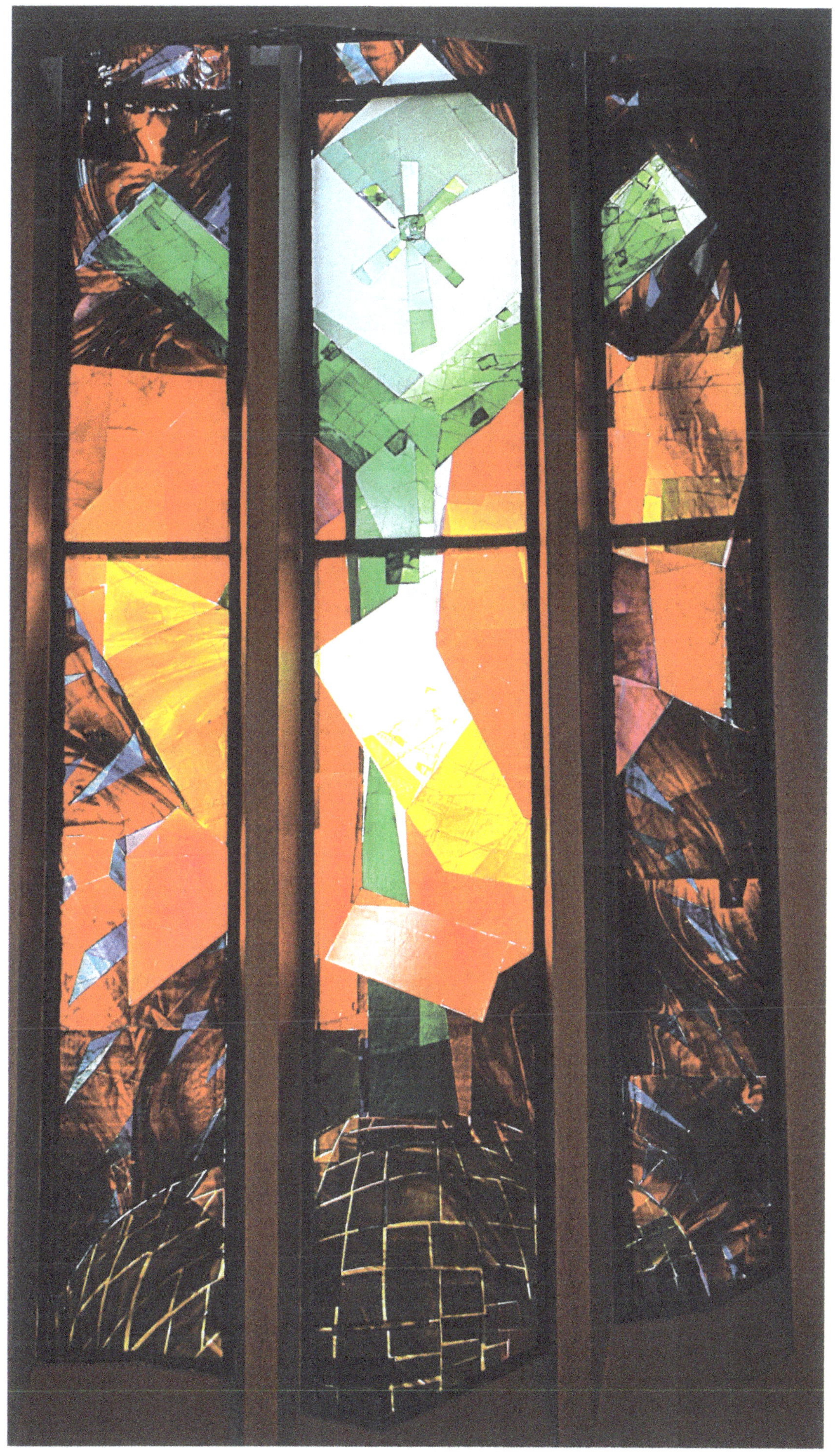

Plate 40

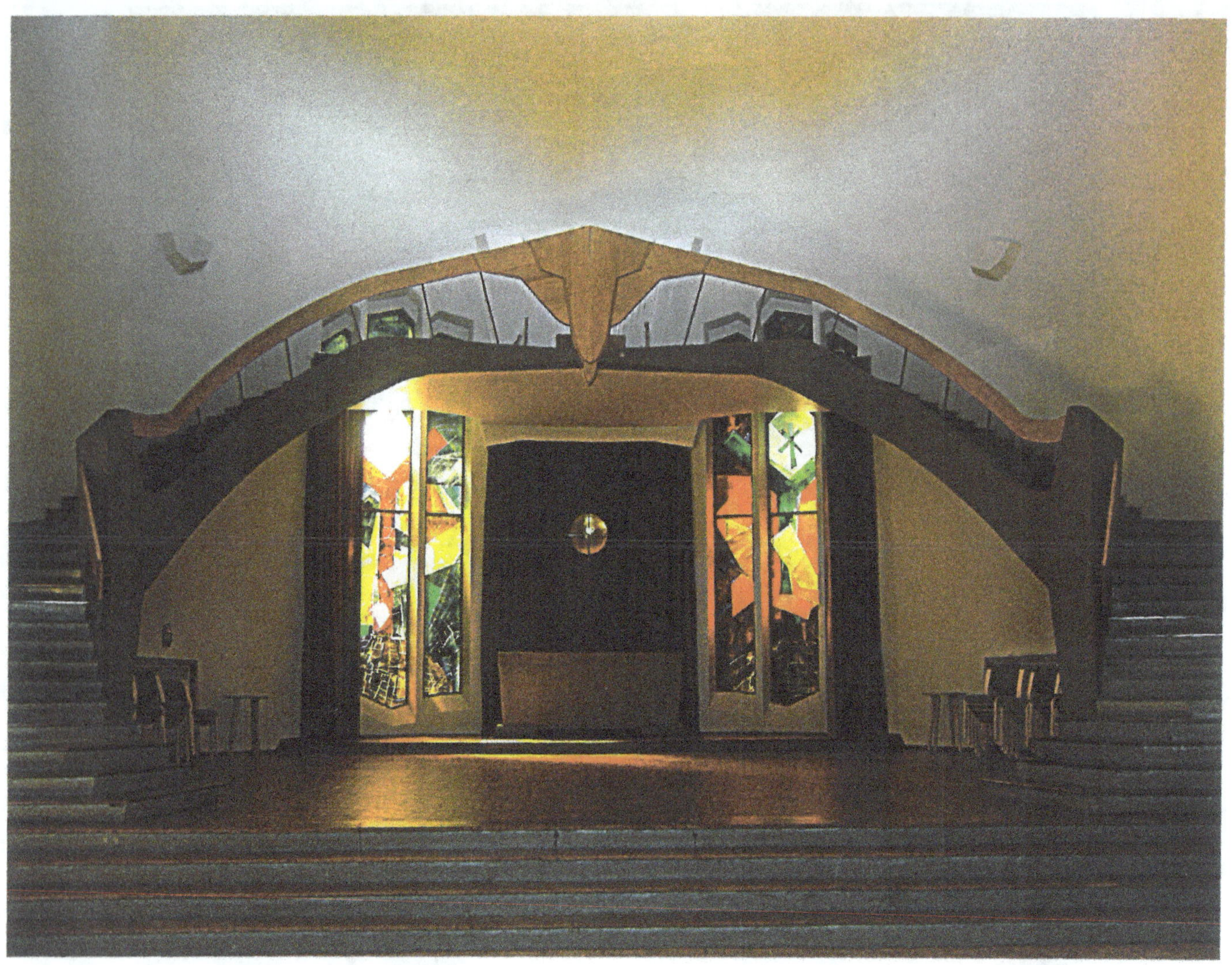

Plate 41

often depicted the cross in Crucifixion scenes as a Tau cross (e.g., Rogier van der Weyden, *The Descent from the Cross,* 1435 Museo del Prado, Madrid; *The Crucifixion,* 1445 Kunsthistorisches Museum, Vienna). More significant perhaps is the fact that Christ's body would have assumed a Y shape given that his wrists (not hands) were nailed to the horizontal cross beam. Whether or not there was a mercy seat and/or a platform upon which Christ's feet rested, the weight of his body would have led to a Y shape configuration. So, is Gross alluding here to Christ's agony on the cross?

An intriguing feature of the windows is that the longer one looks at them the more the various shapes seem to dissolve into a series of columnar shaped quartz crystals. This may reflect the longstanding belief in some Camphill communities that quartz has powerful metaphysical qualities, able not only to direct and amplify energy but also to facilitate physical and spiritual healing and in promoting meditation.

The two Y shapes are presented in the primary and complementary colours of red and green. Being set against the background colours of blue, mauve and brown has the effect of bringing both forward. There is a sense in which we appear to be presented with the most pure form of Cubist abstraction where shapes assume a three-dimensional appearance. Should any cultural connotation be attached to these two colours? Are we to take it that red signifies passion, strength, energy, heat and blood, whilst green suggest fertility, vigour, renewal and creativity? Both Y figures appear to be resting either on the top of a hill or on part of a globe. Is the allusion here to Calvary or to the world? Or both?

Camphill co-workers, like the Benedictine monks of Pluscarden Abbey, never fail to be amazed at the spectacular beauty of stained glass windows constructed with *dalles de verre* when the rays of the sun light upon them. The changing quality of the light during the course of the day and season produces quite different optical effects. Unlike many stained glass windows, which are either two-dimensional representations of biblical scenes or memorials of some kind, the abstract and three-dimensional nature of the Camphill Hall windows brings them to life and makes a strong, memorable and vibrant visual impact.

Sketches

As further demonstration of Gross' great versatility, it is worth looking at a selection of drawings which have been taken from his sketch diaries. (Plates 42–52) One of the advantages of being an artist-in-residence in a residential school was that Gross had long holidays. Apart from the many sketches of places visited there are a number of appealing portraits, which are drawn with great economy and style, and revealing an uncharacteristic degree of completeness. It is clear from his sketch diaries that he kept for most of his time at Camphill that he travelled extensively throughout and beyond Europe. In order to have a measure of freedom and to keep costs to a minimum — two Camphill qualities he quickly absorbed — he bought a succession of second-hand VW Caravanette camper vans! By disposition it is unlikely that Gross would have enjoyed the carefully choreographed itineraries of conventional holidays.

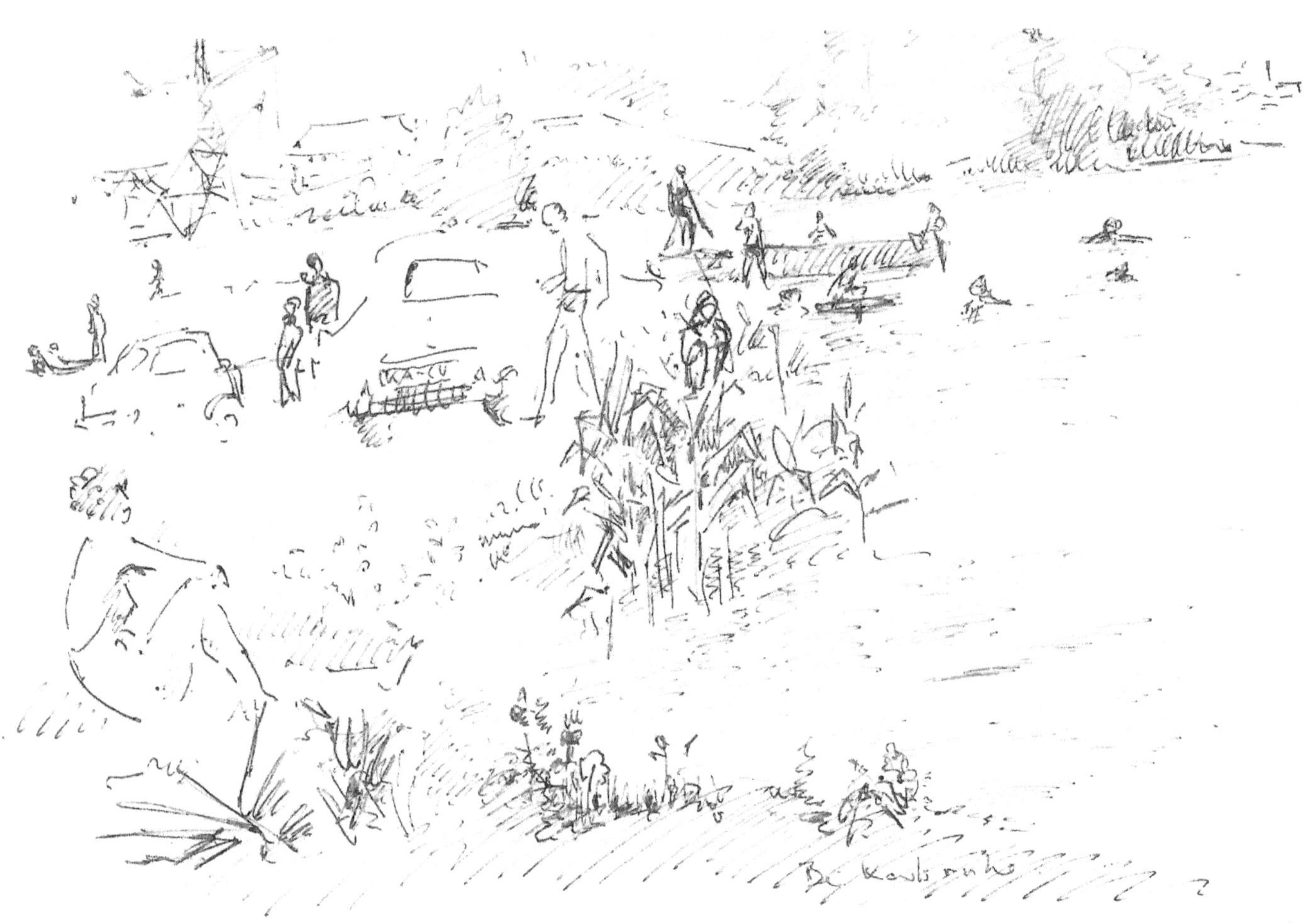

Plate 42

Plate 43

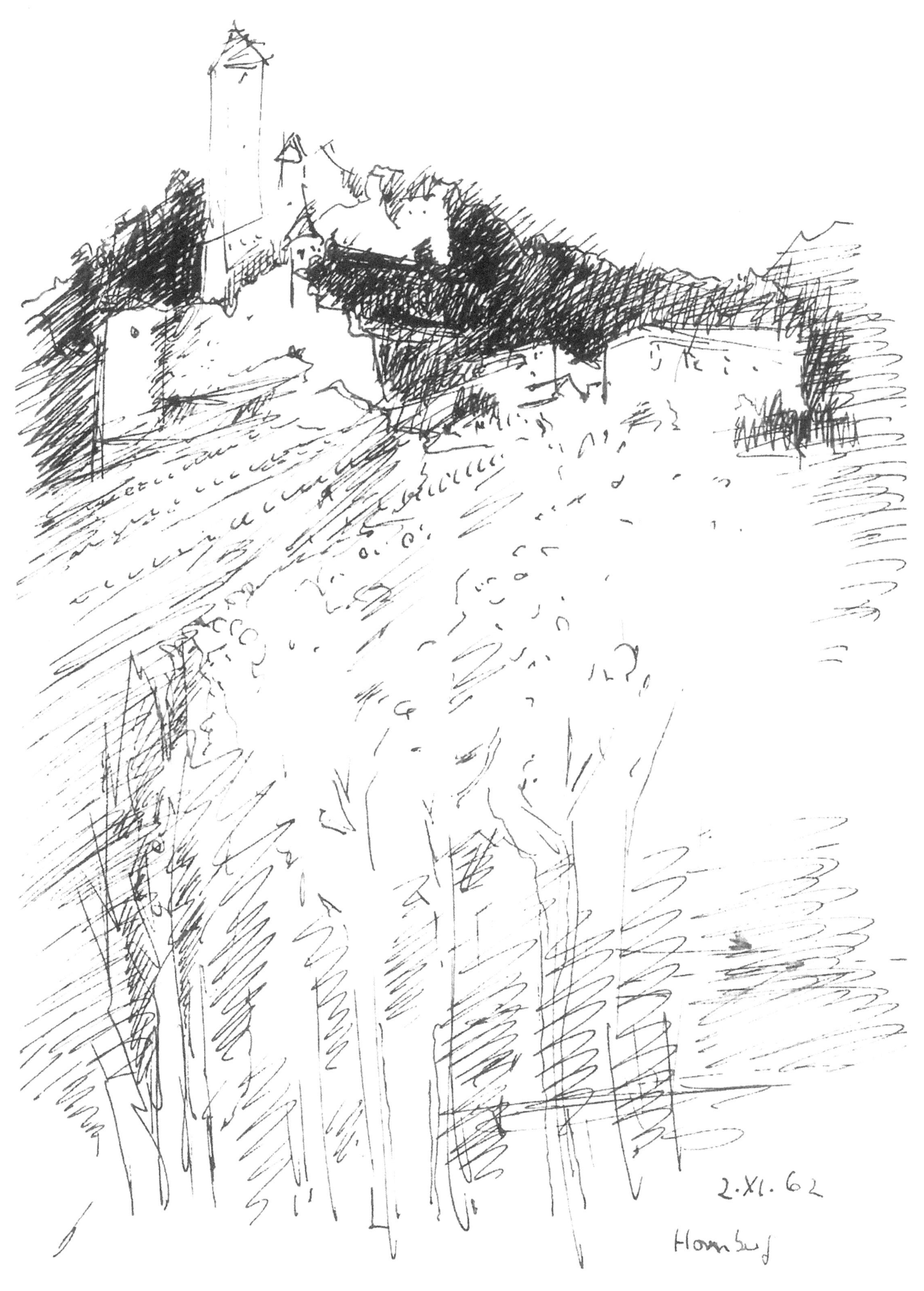
2.XI.62
Hornburg

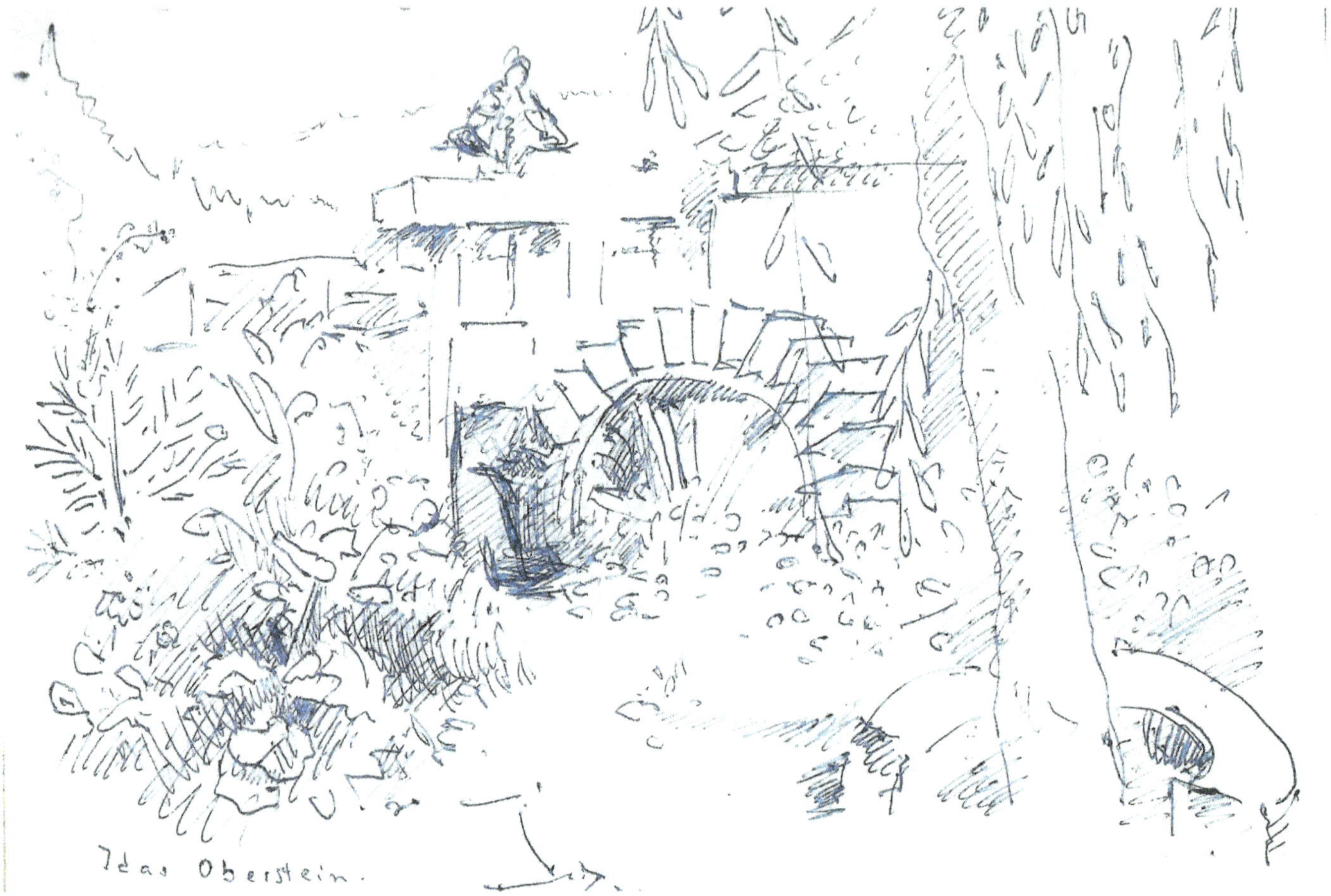

Plate 44

Plate 45

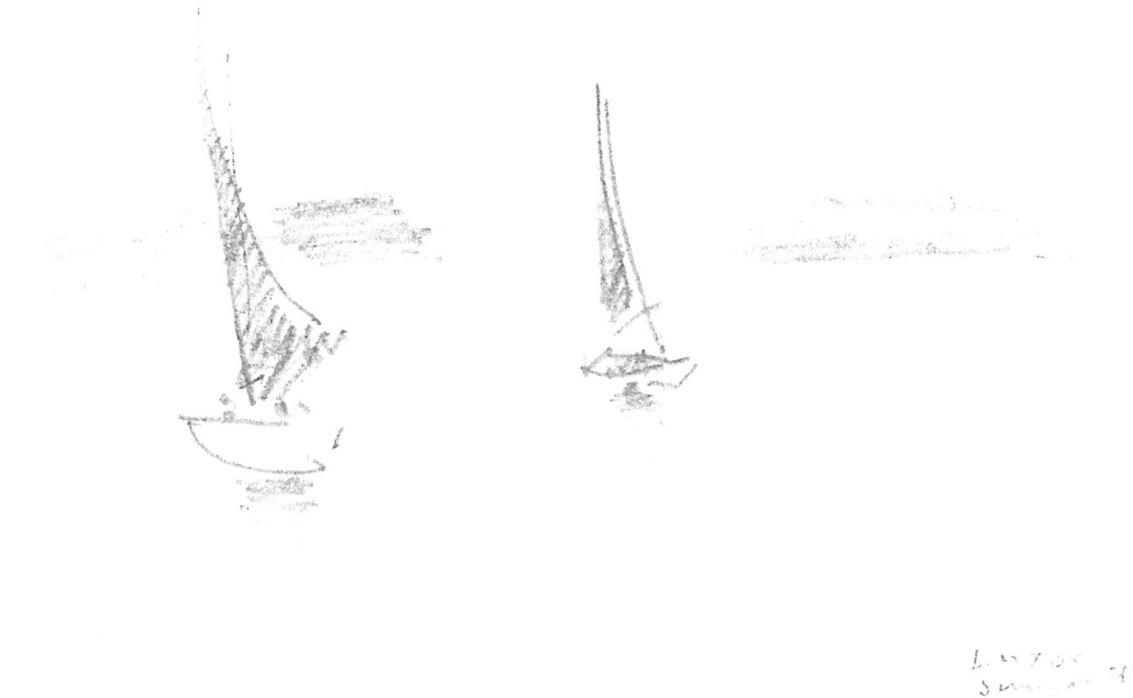

Plate 46

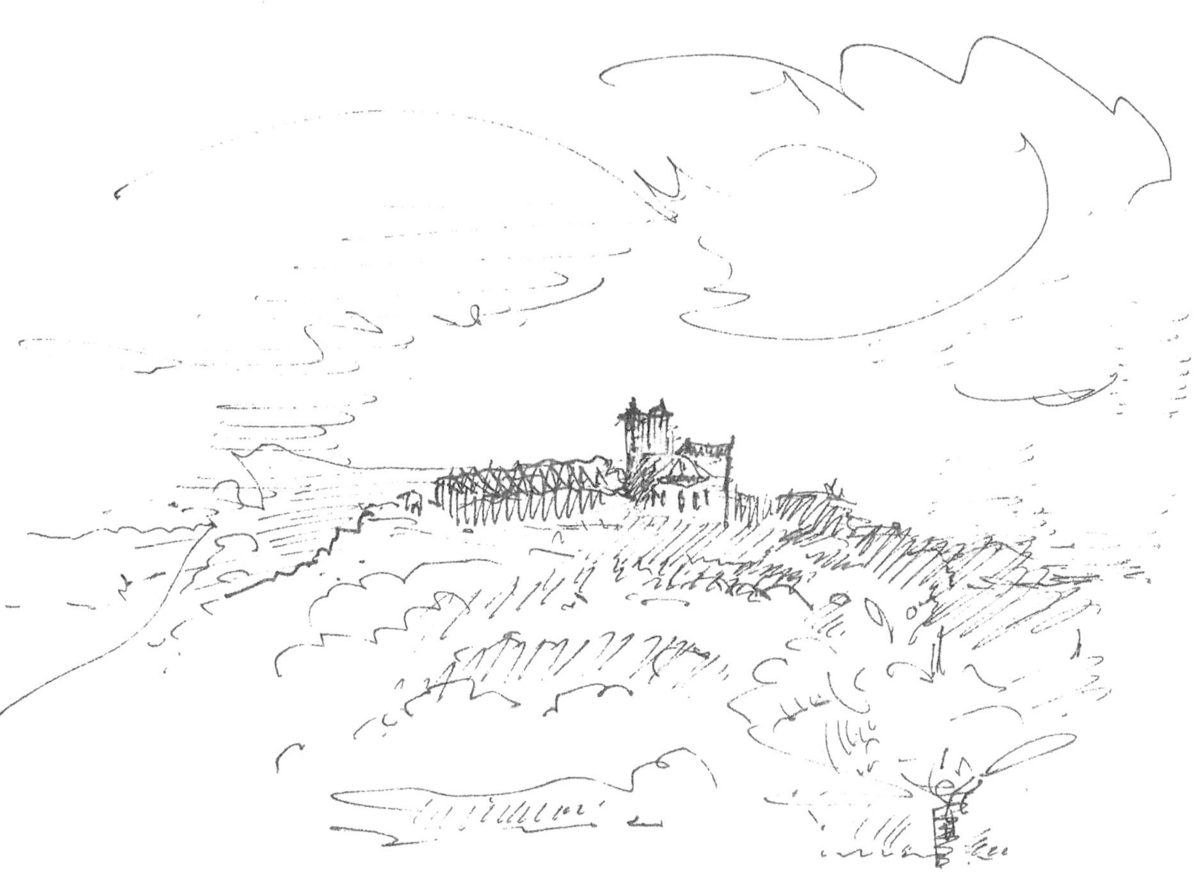

Plate 47

There are two intriguing entries in his sketch diaries. The first relates to Richard (Rab) Butler, Mollie and Stephen Courtauld, who it would appear he had met on the Isle of Mull, whilst on holiday there. It is known that Rab Butler had a holiday home in Calgary Bay — Frachadil House — where he spent twenty summers. Rab Butler was one of the most distinguished British politicians of the 20th century and was Deputy Prime Minister to no fewer than three Prime Ministers. His abiding legacy was the 1944 Education Act which laid the foundations of the modern British educational system. What is of particular interest is the fact that Butler was judged to be one of the better do-it-yourself parliamentary painters which included, among others, Winston Churchill. It is also known that resulting from his first marriage to Sydney Courtauld, the textile heiress, he inherited a priceless collection of French art including paintings by Renoir, Cézanne and Manet. Whilst there is no hint in the diaries of the content of their conversations, it would be very surprising if Gross and Butler had not discussed their mutual interest in art.

One portrait sketch is of particular interest. It is of Julia (Rosenthal), a young girl with cerebral palsy. (Plate 48) At the age of five Julia had been referred to a Camphill community in Gloucestershire — Thornbury Park — which at that time specialized in the education and treatment of children with cerebral palsy. Julia was the daughter of Harry and Marjorie Rosenthal. Harry Rosenthal had been one of the leading Bauhaus architects, who because of the introduction of the Nuremberg Race Laws in the 1930s, had to leave his native Germany along with more than 130 other Jewish architects and begin life afresh in Palestine (Warhaftig, 2007). Many of these architects, including Rosenthal, left behind them in Germany significant buildings that were at that time central to the urban image of Berlin. For example, Rosenthal was responsible for the design of Arnold Zweig's studio in Berlin Charlottenburg. Zweig had been a strong opponent of Hitler and the Nazi Party, co-editor of the anti-fascist magazine *World Stage*. He was exiled by the Nazis in 1935. After the war he returned from Palestine to East Germany and served as president of the German Academy of Arts (1950–1953). He is best known for his novels *Education Before Verdun* (1935), *The Crowning of a King* (1937) and *The Axe of Wandsbek* (1947).

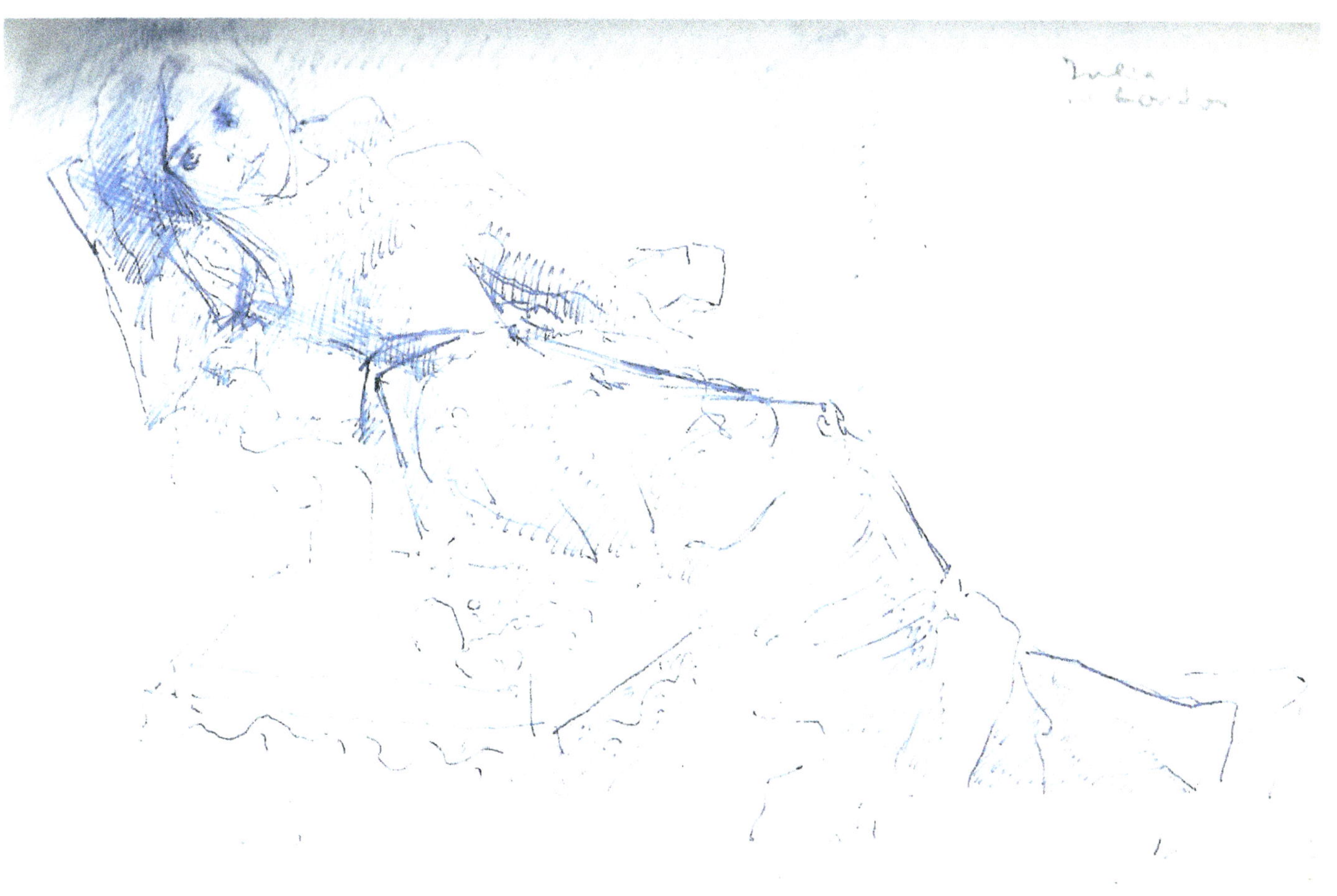

Plate 48

Upon arriving in their new desert home in Palestine, Rosenthal and the other Jewish architects set about laying the foundations of a new society with astonishing energy, despite being completely unaccustomed to the climate, the culture or the language. They were responsible for the construction of kibbutzim, housing developments in villages and cities, hospitals, schools, universities, theatres and administrative buildings (Claus, 2006). To this day, Tel Aviv still has the largest collection of buildings built in the Bauhaus style, anywhere in the world. Records of Rosenthal's architectural work are now lodged alongside those of Ludwig Mies van der Rohe (1886–1969) and Hermann Muthesius (1861–1927) in the Architecture Archive Department of the Academy of Arts in Berlin.

The day before his death in 1966 Harry Rosenthal was able to celebrate the fact that Julia, who had spent some time in a psychiatric hospital after leaving Thornbury Park and who had refused to eat or drink whilst in hospital, had been invited to Camphill for three weeks. Those three weeks eventually turned into 20 years, for Julia remained in Aberdeen until her death in 1985. Marjorie Rosenthal, Julia's mother, who had trained as a social worker went on to play a very important role in giving advice and support to parents of children who were subsequently admitted to Camphill. She, like Gross, later made her home on the Camphill Murtle Estate.

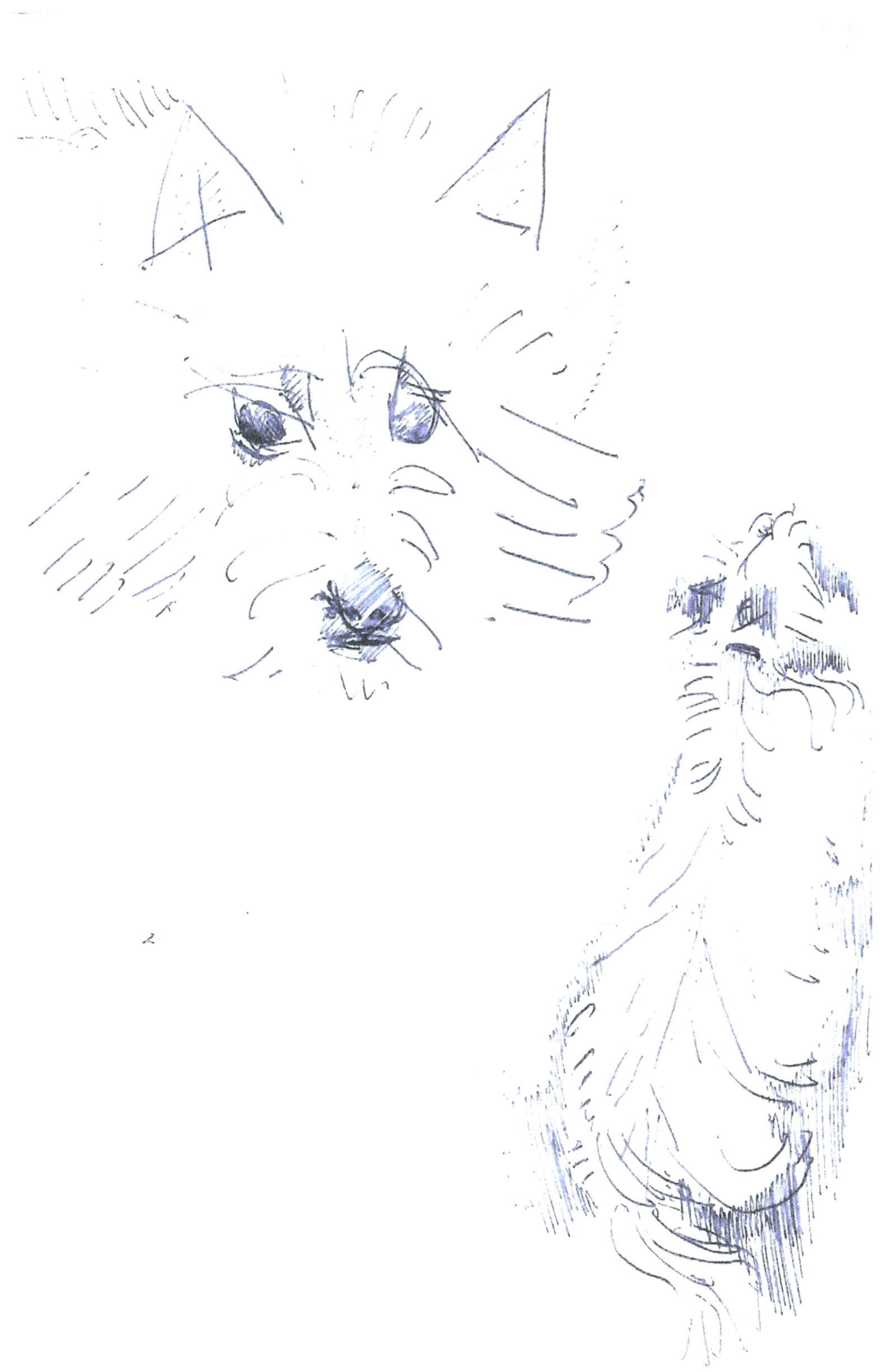

Plate 49

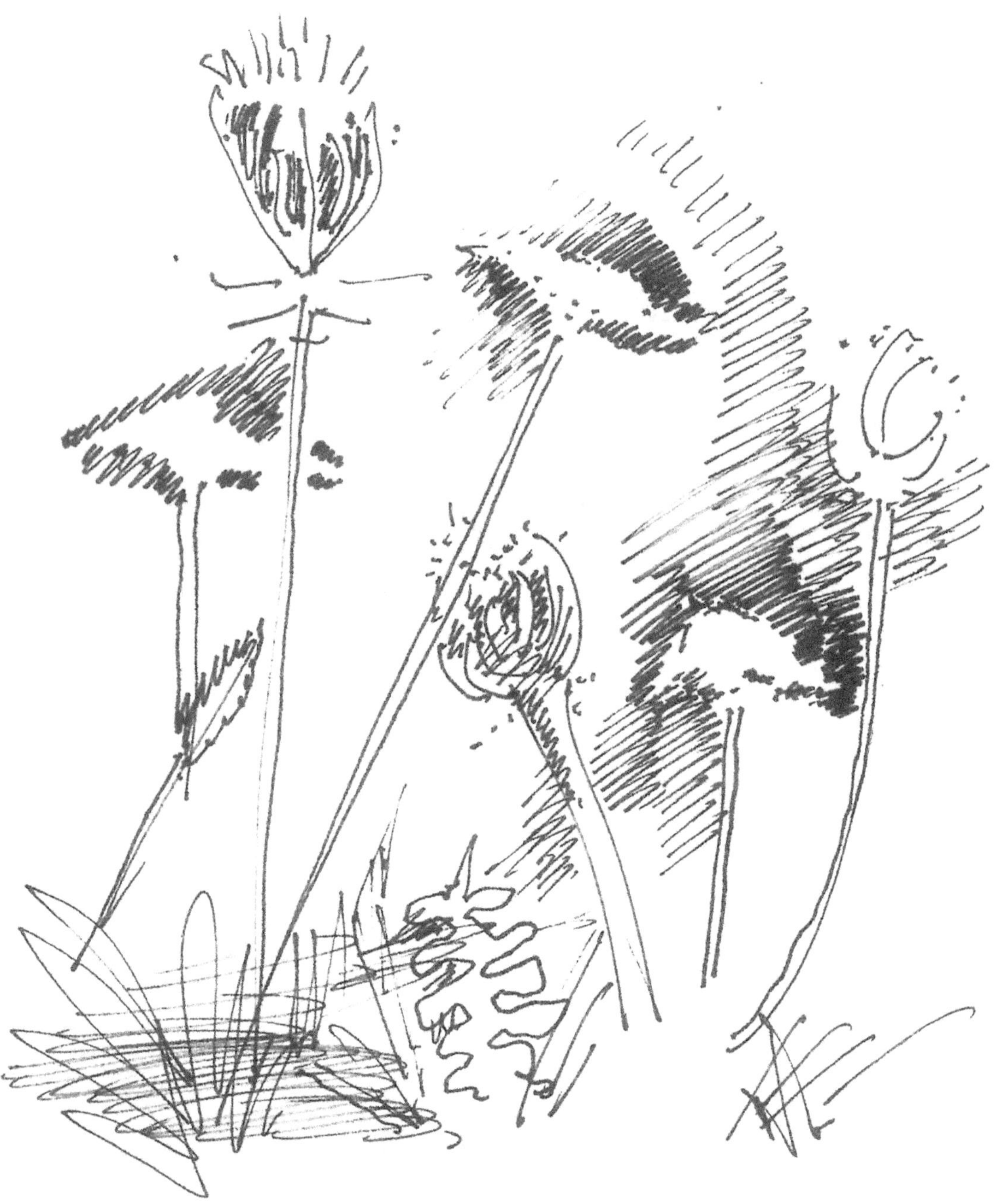

Plate 50

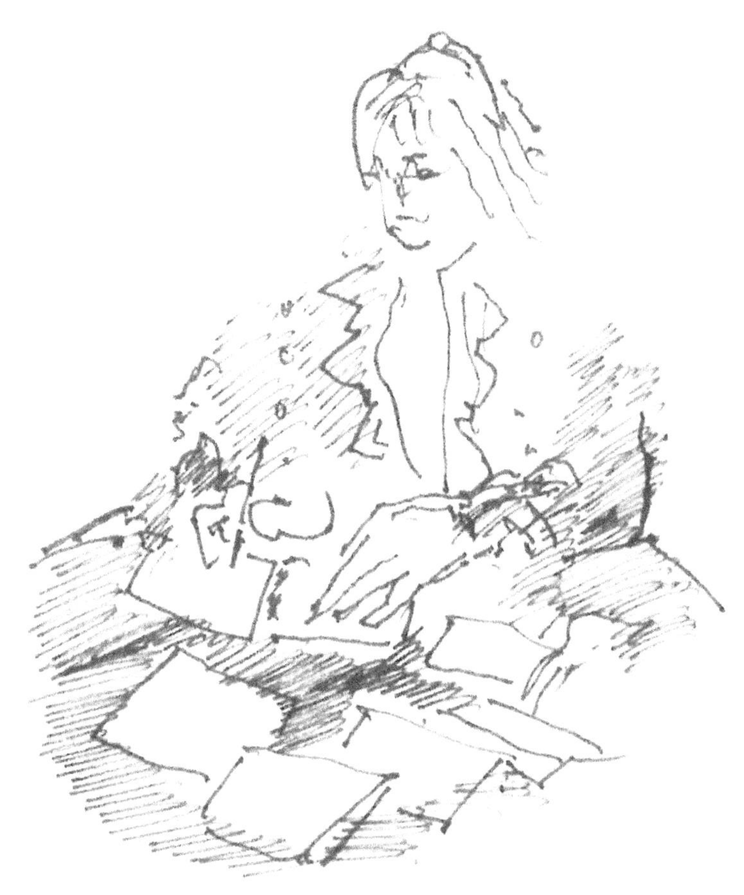

20.10.84.
G.

Plate 51

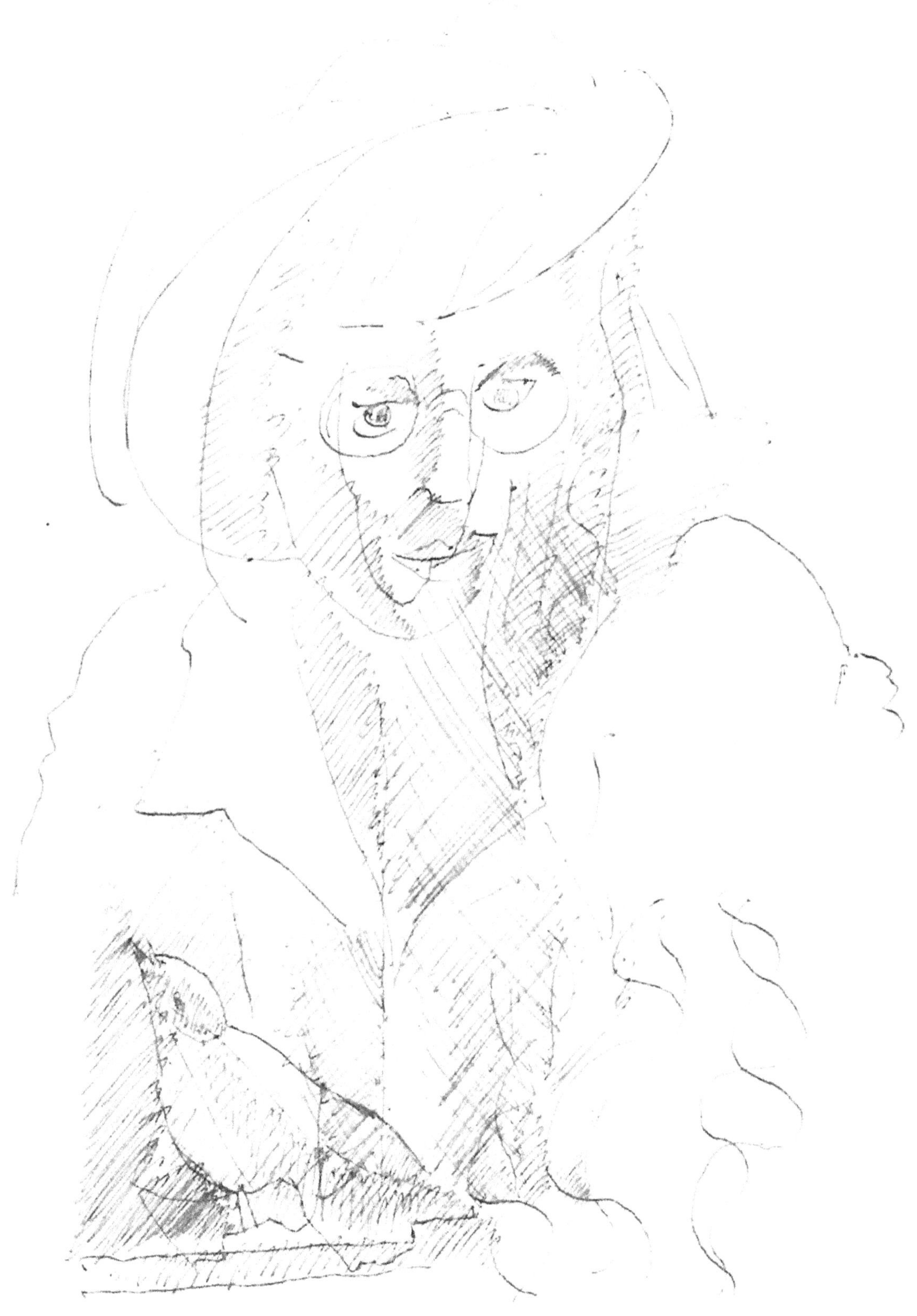

Plate 52

10. Conclusion

Whilst Camphill communities have sometimes been characterised as possessing some of the features of a lay religious order, it is unlikely that Gross' paintings would have made such an impact had they taken the form of the stark and explicitly religious works painted immediately after the war. However, in the paintings which have been discussed, his deeply held spirituality is expressed in a subtle and appealing manner and language that is more likely to engage and impact upon the viewer. Most of Gross' paintings can be viewed as meditation pieces, for they were hung in different houses and meeting rooms in the Camphill community, and many would have been the focal point in a room. In other words, they were positioned in such a way to challenge people to contemplate their meaning. In that respect it could be argued that we are returning to a much earlier tradition when art was a largely ecclesiastical monopoly. Most paintings were destined for churches and monasteries, to promote and strengthen spiritual thought and commitment in both clerical and lay viewers.

Gross' artist-in-residentship at Camphill was unlike the often short-term, high profile, media conscious and externally funded projects, where the artist has a limited opportunity to get the know the population with whom s/he resides, to identify the issues that need to be addressed and to find the right language and medium in which to communicate. Only with the passage of time did Gross gain the confidence and insights necessary to communicate with those with whom he lived and worked. In other words, the current concept of the artist-in-residence is not best served by its often transitory nature.

Karl König had seen the role of long-term community-oriented art as a way of heightening the social consciousness of those living in Camphill. Today organisational theorists along with holistic educators recognise that 'healthy' organisations tend to evolve where an environment has been created which facilitates the development of the 'reflective practitioner': someone who, at regular intervals, looks back at the work they do, and the work process, and considers how they can improve. Gross' art was directed to that end. It is the antithesis of propagandist art that celebrates and demands conformity and uniformity.

The time is long overdue for Gross' great talents as a sculptor and painter to be more generally recognised. Whilst the content of his paintings has a particular resonance within the context of a Camphill community, their message should be communicated to a far wider audience. Why is his work not more widely known? Part of the answer lies in his decision to spend the latter part of his life working modestly as an artist-in-residence in a small school in the North East of Scotland remote from the artistic and intellectual heartlands of Paris, Berlin and New York. When Gross came to Scotland, he abandoned a career in the ordinary sense of the word, for a large part of a professional artist's life is often devoted to seeking a market. Freed from concerns about remuneration, Gross no longer saw his works as commodities for sale. It was in this Camphill community that he experienced one of his most productive periods and it was here that he died on 1 September 1988. In his interview with William Dunbar of the *Scottish Sunday Express* Gross indicated that he did not want to be like other artists who just played at being artists and sat in their ivory towers imitating others: "I felt the whole conception of artists in the Western world was wrong — that doing must replace philosophising about art" (Dunbar, 1963).

It is not unusual for a full appreciation of the unique qualities of an artist to be delayed until some time after death. Such is the case with Hermann Gross. It is hoped that this monograph demonstrates his supreme technical ability, extraordinary versatility and creative imagination. As Aline Louchheim, the doyenne of New York art critics, noted in 1951, Gross was not only a true descendant of the German Expressionist school but also someone who used that art form to communicate a powerful spiritual message which was relevant to contemporary society. His art continues to communicate that message.

Bibliography

Acton, M. (2004) *Learning to Look at Modern Art*, Routledge, London.

Baal-Teshuva, J. (2003) *Chagall: 1887–1985*. Taschen, Cologne: 276.

Buchanan, M. (2006) Rhode Island School of Design, Providence, Rhode Island; email message to author, July 27, 2006.

City of Philadelphia Department of Public Property: The Great Mother & The Great Doctor. http://www.phila.gov/property/vp_art_mother.html

Claus, S. (2006) *Plastische Architektur. Das Werk des Architekten: Harry Rosenthal (1892–1966)*, GVA-Vertriebsgemeinschaft.

Der Kurier, 1957, January 13. Extract held in Hermann Gross Archive, Aberdeen.

Dimond, S. (2007) Manchester, Vermont: email message to author, July 26, 2007.

Dimond, S. (2008) Personal communication, March 25.

Dunbar, W. (1963) 'The teachers who never tire of giving,' *Scottish Sunday Express*, October 27.

Ehlen, B. (1989) 'Obituary to Hermann Gross,' *Camphill Correspondence*: March/April.

Ehlen, B. (2006) Wickersdorf: email message to author, June 13, 2006.

Ehlen, B. (2006) Wickersdorf: email message to author, July 21, 2006.

Gebhard, V. (1988) 'An appreciation of Hermann Gross the artist,' in *Hermann Gross: an artist in a community of children with special needs.* (Exhibition catalogue, Aberdeen).

Geider, S. (2008) Aberdeen: email message to author, January 29, 2008.

Gross, H. (1962) Mescher Studio address, The Hermann Trust Archive, Aberdeen.

Gross, H. (1989) quoted in 'Obituary issue,' *Camphill Correspondence*: March/April issue. Unpaginated.

Harbison, C. (1995) *The Mirror of the Artist: Northern Renaissance Art in its historical context*, Prentice Hall, New Jersey.

Haustein, H. (1991) 'Friend, painter and sculptor,' in *Hermann Gross*, ed. Peter Schirmer Unpublished document, Aberdeen.

Hillers, M. (2006) *A Woman in Berlin: eight weeks in the conquered city — a diary.* Virago Press: London.

Howe, E. and P. (1988) Untitled contribution to *Hermann Gross: an artist in a community of children with special needs.* (Exhibition catalogue, Aberdeen).

Imhof-Cardinal, C. (2008) Aberdeen: email message to author, January 24, 2008.

Jackson, R. (2006) 'The Camphill Movement: the vision of Karl König,' *Encounter: Education for Meaning and Social Justice*: 19(2), 45–48.

Jackson, R. (2006) (Ed.) *Holistic Special Education: Camphill Principles and Practice,* Edinburgh, Floris Books.

Jackson, R. (2008) 'Camphill: The Moravian Dimension,' *Camphill Correspondence*: 1–3. January/February.

Kandinsky, W. (1979) *Concerning the Spiritual in Art,* Dover Books, New York.

Kashmiry, K. (2007) Smithsonian Archives of Modern Art, Washington, DC: email message to author, July 23, 2007.

Knight, D. (1999) 'Why we enjoy condemning sentimentality: a meta-aesthetic perspective,' *The Journal of Aesthetics and Art Criticism*: 57(4), 411–420.

Kovic, R. (1976) *Born on The Fourth of July,* McGraw Hill, New York.

Maier, H. (2004) 'Rhythmicity: a powerful force for experiencing unity and personal connections,' *Journal of Child and Youth Care Work,* (2004): 8, 7–14.

Morell, R. (2007) Winchester, Virginia: email message to author, September 14, 2007.

Pioch, N. (2002) 'Wassily Kandinsky: Improvisation 31 (Sea Battle),' 31 July 2002 http://www/ibiblio.org/wm/paint/auth/kandinsky/sea-battle/

Plievier, T. (1948) *Stalingrad,* Appleton-Century-Crofts, Inc., New York.

Rath, H. (1963) 'My art is compulsive,' *American Artist*: 34–39, 76. September.

Ravetz, D. (1991) *Hermann Gross* ed. Peter Schirmer, Unpublished document, Aberdeen.

Remarque, E. (2005) *All Quiet on the Western Front,* Vintage Books, London.

Ringborn, S. (1985) 'Kandinsky and 'Der Blaue Reiter',' in *German Art in the 20th Century: Paintings and Sculpture 1905–1985,* ed. C. Joachimides, N. Rosenthal and W. Schmied, Royal Academy of Arts Prestel-Verlag, London: 429–431.

Rosenthal, M. (1989) 'Obituary to Hermann Gross,' *Camphill Correspondence*: March/April.

Ryback, T. (2003) 'Hitler's Forgotten Library: The Man, His Books and His Search for God,' *The Atlantic Monthly,* May.

Salon D'Automne, Paris. (2006): email message to author, June 15, 2006.

Sander, M. (1988) 'Hermann Gross and his art,' in *Hermann Gross: an artist in a community of children with special needs.* Exhibition catalogue, Aberdeen.

Schirmer, P. (1991) *Hermann Gross,* ed. Peter Schirmer Unpublished document, Aberdeen.

Schlegel, G. (1999) 'Obituary issue,' *Camphill Correspondence*: March/April issue. Unpaginated.

Schnell, M. (1989) 'Obituary issue,' *Camphill Correspondence*): March/April issue. Unpaginated.

Schnell, M. (2006): Aberdeen: email message to author, May 21, 2006.

Schnell, M. (2008): Aberdeen: email message to author, February 19, 2008.

Schwarzwaldzeitung (1956) November 26. Extract held in Hermann Gross Archive, Aberdeen.

Schwarzwald Bote (1956) November 26. Extract held in Hermann Gross Archive, Aberdeen.

Telegraf (1957) January 13. Extract held in Hermann Gross Archive, Aberdeen.

The Concord Monitor (1952) July 1. Extract held in Hermann Gross Archive, Aberdeen.

Throm, J. (2006) Smithsonian Archives of Modern Art, Washington, DC: email message to author, May 31, 2006.

Toepfer, K. (1992) 'Nudity and modernity in German dance, 1910–1930,' *Journal of the History of Sexuality*: 3(1) 58–108.

Toepfer, K. (1997) *Empire of Ecstasy: Nudity and Movement in German Body Culture: 1910–1935*, University of California Press, Berkeley.

von Berswordt-Wallrabe, K, R. Erbentraut and R. Weingart. (2001) *Otto Manigk 1902–1972: Malerei*, Staatliches Museum, Schwerin.

Wagner, C. (1991) *Hermann Gross*, ed. Peter Schirmer, Unpublished document, Aberdeen.

Warhaftig, M. (2007) *They Laid the Foundations: Lives and Works of German-Speaking Jewish Architects in Palestine 1918–1948*, Wasmuth, Tübingen.

Wasmuth, G. (1929) *Lexicon der Baukunst*, Verlag Ernst Wasmuth, Berlin.

Wasmuth, E. (1946) *Blaise Pascal: Über die Religion und über einige andere Gegenstände. (Pensées)*, Schneider, Heidelberg.

Zweig, A. (1935) *Education before Verdun,* Viking Press, New York.

Zweig, A. (1937) *The Crowning of a King,* Viking Press, New York.

Zweig, A. (1947) *The Axe of Wandsbek,* Viking Press, New York.

Index

Aberdeen 10, 49, 61, 78
—, Art Gallery 8, 10
—, University 9
—, Marischal Museum 9
—, School of Education 9
Accademia Italia delle Arti e del Lavoro 35
Acton, Mary 49, 113
Africa (Benin) 69
Alexander II of Scotland 94
Alloa Parish Church 95
America 34, 47
American Artist 35
Ansbach 84
Apollinaire, Guillaume 20
Apollo Programme 37
Art Digest 44, 46
Art News 44, 46
Athena 92
Atlantic Wall 29
Austria 53

Baal-Teshuva, Jacob 61, 113
—, *Chagall: 1887–1985*
Baden 84
Baden-Württemberg 11, 34
Baltic Sea coast 35
Bande à Schnegg 20
Barrault, Jean-Louis 24
Basel 25
Bauhaus 31, 104, 106
Benedictine community 94, 99
Benin 69
Bergson, Henri 49
Berlin 7, 19, 25, 32, 47f, 67, 106, 112
—, Akademie der Bildenen Kunste 35
—, Alexanderplatz 25
—, Berliner Kunstakademie 35
—, *Der Kurier* 48, 113
—, Galerie Wasmuth 48
—, Landsbergerstrasse 25, 32
—, Olympic Stadium 19
—, *Telegraf* 48, 115
Bible 45
Blackbottom 14
Black Forest 11
Blake, William 44
Bolshoi Ballet 16
Boncompagni, Princess 39
Brancusi, Constantin 7, 24, 70f
Braque, Georges 23f, 27, 58
Buchanan, Melissa 19, 113
Burrows, Carlyle 43
Butler, Richard (Rab) 104

Cagnes-sur-Mer 23
Calvary 32, 99
Camphill 7, 49, 53–56, 58, 77, 79, 82, 84, 86, 92, 96, 99, 106, 111f
Camphill Hall 49, 61, 92, 94f, 99
—, *Michael* 49, 92
—, *Raphael* 49, 92
—, *A Praying Man* 49, 92
Camphill Movement 49, 61
Camphill Rudolf Steiner School 9, 48, 78, 86
Carné, Marcel 24
Caravaggio 63
Casablanca 16
Casals, Pablo 55
Catholic Church 32
Cézanne, Paul 67, 104
Chagall, Marc 7, 24, 29, 58, 61
Charleston 14
Christ 29, 32, 41, 46, 61, 63, 77, 98
Christianity 31, 39, 41, 44, 61
Churchill, Winston 104
Claus, Sylvia 106, 113
Cocteau, Jean 23
Connoway, Jay 38

Courtauld, Mollie 104
Courtauld, Stephen 104
Courtauld, Sydney 104
Cubism 69, 70, 99
Deauville 23
Derain, André 24, 67
De Solidor, Suzy 22–24
Dietschy, Karl 25
Dimond, Scott 65, 74, 113
Dorset, Vermont 36–39
Du Bois, Guy Pene 38
Dunbar, William 27, 53, 112f

Eardley, Joan 78f
Eastern Front 32
Eastern mysticism 16
Easter Island (Oceania) 69, 71
Ehlen, Bernd 11, 22, 24, 28, 113
Einsatzstab Reichsleiter Rosenberg (ERR) 27
Elektra 43, 47
Episcopalian church 65
Exorcism painting 69
Exxon 39
Eye of Horus 70

Fahkry, Princess 39
France 7, 11, 22f, 34
Frank, Inge 16
Freud, Sigmund 49
Freudenstadt 34, 47
—, Art House 34
—, Stadthaus 34, 47
Friedrichs, Hildegard 22, 25

Gebhard, Volker 55, 95, 113
Geider, Stefan 56f, 113
German Air Force 7, 57
German Expressionism 42, 45, 48, 112
German Sixth Army 25
Germany 14, 16, 25, 28, 32, 35, 45, 47, 53, 92, 104
Gestapo 25
Glasgow 78
Goering, Hermann 27f, 40
Goya 78
Greek mythology 69
Greyhound Bus 39
Gross, Hermann
—, *Abraham Tempted to Offer Isaac for Sacrifice* 46
—, *Christ crowned with Thorns*
—, *Crucifixion* 42, 44
—, *Doppelgesicht* 47
—, *Entombment* 42, 46
—, *Jacob's Dream* 46
—, *The Descent from the Cross* 46
—, *The Malefactor to the Right of Christ* 44
—, *The Malefactor to the Left of Christ* 44
—, *The Inspiration* 44f
—, *The Legionnaire and the Boy* 74
—, *The Resurrection* 42, 46
—, *Touch Me Not* 46
—, *Under the Cross* 46

Harbison, Craig 32, 113
Harlequin 67, 84
Hauser, Kaspar 83f
Haustein, Hans 14, 22, 25, 47, 67, 113
Haustein, Paul 16, 19
Heilpädagogik 92
Hitler, Adolph 16, 29
Hillers, Martha 25, 113
Howe, Elizabeth 54, 113
Howe, Peter 54, 113
Hurricanes 28
Heinkels 28

Ikora design 19
Imhof-Cardinal, Catherine 57, 113

Jackson, Robin 7–9, 53, 61, 113f

Kanalküste 29
Kandinsky, Wassily 42, 49, 53, 59, 114
Kashmiry, Kathryn 38f, 42, 114
Knight, Deborah 77f, 114
Kokoschka, Oscar 42, 45
Kollsman, Julie 38

Kollsman, Paul 37f
Kollsman Window 37
König, Karl 49, 53f, 61, 78, 111
Kovic, Ron, 25, 114

La commedia dell'arte 67
Lahr 11
Lake Zurich 49, 53
Laserstein, Lotte 35
Laurencin, Marie 7
Leipzig 14
Loewenstein, Laszlo 16
Loewy, Raymond 39
London 78
Lorre, Peter 16
Louchheim, Aline 43, 63, 112
Lucky Strike 39
Luftwaffe 27f
—, Propaganda Kompanie 3
Luther, Martin 32

Macbeth Gallery 38f, 41f, 44f
Macbeth, William 39
Macdiarmid, Hugh 95
Maier, Henry 92, 114
Maltese Falcon 16
Manchester, Vermont 36f
Manchester Journal 38
Manet, Édouard 92, 104
Manigk, Otto 35
Matisse, Henri 24, 27
Masks 58, 67–70, 74
McIntyre, Robert 38f, 41, 43
McLellan, Sadie 95
Melville, Jennifer 8
Messerschmitts 28
Milstein, Nathan Mrs 39
Modigliani, Amedeo 24, 29
Moravian Church 61
Morayshire 94
Morrell, Ron 37, 114
Moscow 25
Munch, Edvard 35
Munich 37
—, Playhouse 14
Muthesius, Hermann 106
Myra design 19

Nacktkultur 14
NASA 37
Nashua, New Hampshire 36
Naess, Erling 39
Nazi 25, 27–29, 44, 46, 104
—, Party 25, 104
—, Regime 25, 31f, 53
Newton, Eric 78
Newton Dee 49
New York 7, 38, 44, 47, 63, 113
—, Brooklyn Museum 36
—, European School of Fine Art 38
—, 20 Fifth Avenue 38, 41
—, Metropolitan Museum of Art 36, 71
—, Public Library 36
—, Waldorf Astoria 38
—, Washington Square 38
New York Herald Tribune 43–45
New York Times 42–45, 63
Nietzsche, Friedrich 49
Noh 79, 82
—, Actors 79
—, Masks 82
—, Musicians 79
—, Tradition 79
Normandy 29
Northern Renaissance Art 32
Nuremberg 82
Nuremberg Race Laws 104

Obergefreiter 28
Oceania (Easter Island) 69, 71
Occidental occultism 16

Palestime 104f
Paris 7, 10f, 20, 22–25, 27, 29, 34, 40, 57f, 61, 70f, 112
—, 48 Avenue des Gobelins 22
—, Boîte de Nuit 23
—, Jeu de Paume Museum 27
—, L'Academie de la Grande Chaumière 20

—, L'École des Beaux-Arts 20
—, Montparnasse 22, 24
—, Musée National d'Art Moderne 61
—, Salon d'Automne 24, 114
—, Salon de la Société Nationale des Beaux-Arts 20
Parthenon publishing house 14
Pascal 26
Pericles 69
Philadelphia 20, 86
Picasso, Pablo 7, 10, 23f, 27, 57, 67, 69, 70
—, *Les Demoiselles d'Avignon* 69
—, *Pictures on Exhibition* 46
Pierrot 67, 84
Pioch, Nicolas 59, 114
Pleydell-Bouverie, Alice 39
Plievier, Theodor 25
Pluscarden Abbey 94f
Poland 32
Polynesia 71
Post Impressionists 67, 92
Potsdam 35
Pressezeichner 28
Prix de Paris 35

Radio Stuttgart 47
Raemisch, Waldemar 19, 86
Rath, Dolf 34, 36–38
Rath, Hildegard 34–38, 114
Rath, Walter 34, 36–38
Ravetz, Deborah 54, 114
Red Cross 31
Remarque, Erich Maria 25, 114
Rembrandt 63
Renoir 104
Rhode Island School of Design 19
Ringborn, Sixten 53, 114
Rocher, Suzy Louise 23
Rodin, Auguste 20
Roman Catholic Church 65
Rosenthal, Harry 104–6
Rosenthal, Julia 104–6
Rosenthal, Marjory 49, 106, 114
Rouault, Georges 7, 24, 42, 44
Russia 32
Ryback, Timothy 16, 114

Saarinen, Eero 43
Sachlichkeit 35
Sand, Trude 25, 47, 49, 61, 70
Sander, Marianne 55, 114
Saturn I 39
Saturn V 39
Schertel, Ernst 14, 16
Schirmer, Peter 56, 114
Schlegel, Gisela 54f, 114
Schnell, Marga 24, 56, 61, 114
Schwarzwaldzeitung 47, 114
Schwarzwald Bote, 47, 114
Schwerin 35
Scotland 7, 49, 53, 95, 112
Scottish Sunday Express 27, 112
Selby, Viscount 39
Senglaub, Adolph 35
Shah of Persia 19
Shell International 39
Skylab 39
Snow Valley Ski Resort 37
Soutine 29
Southern Vermont Arts Center 36f
Southern Vermont Artists Inc. 37f
Spitfires 28
Spring Awakening 16
Star of David 31
Steiner, Rudolf 49
Stuttgart 11, 37, 46f, 49
—, Atelier House 34
—, Kunstgewerbeschule 11, 16
—, Mescher Studio 48
—, Waldorf School 49

Tel Aviv 106
The Concord Monitor 43, 115
The Guardian 78
The Sun 45
Thiers 22
Throm, Judy 115
Todt Organization 29
Toepfer, Karl 14, 115

Toulouse 20
—, L'École Municipale des Beaux-Arts 20
Traumbühne Schertel 14, 16, 67

USA 25, 34–37, 40, 43f, 47, 65
Usedom 35

Van der Rohe, Ludwig 106
Van der Weyden, Rogier 22, 98
Van Eyck, Jan 32
Van Eyck, Toni 16
Vermont 34, 36, 38f
Victorian art 77
Virgin Mary 65
Von Berswordt-Wallrabe, Kornelia 35, 115
Von Bodenheim, Julie Dorothea Baronin 38
Vosges Mountains 11

Wagner, Caroline 40, 69, 115
Warhaftig, Myra 104, 115
Washington
—, Library of Congress 36
—, Smithsonian Archives of American Art 15
Wasmuth, Ewald 26, 115
Wasmuth, Günther 26, 115
Weimar Republic 28, 31
Western Front 32
Who's Who in American Art 36
Wlérick, Robert 20
Wolf of Badenoch 94
World War II 53
Württembergische Metallfabrik (WMF) 19

Zweig, Arnold 104, 115

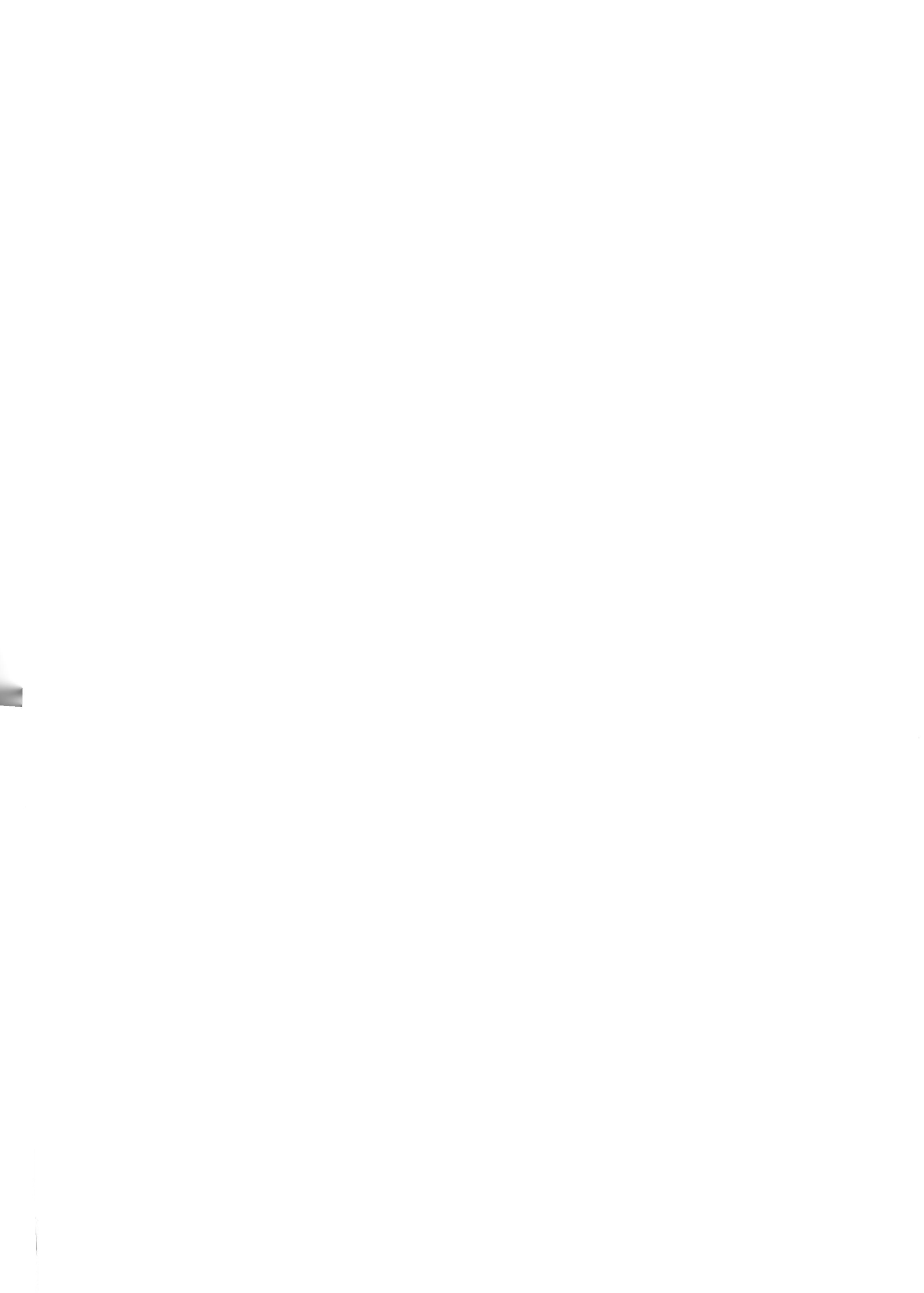

www.ingramcontent.com/pod-product-compliance
Lightning Source LLC
LaVergne TN
LVHW061249100826
845148LV00008B/1074

* 9 7 9 8 3 8 5 2 2 2 2 9 2 *